Augustus Caesar

LANCASTER PAMPHLETS

Augustus Caesar

David Shotter

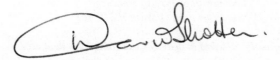

London and New York

First published 1991 by Routledge
11 New Fetter Lane, London EC4P 4EE

Simultaneously published in the USA and Canada by Routledge
a division of Routledge, Chapman and Hall, Inc.
29 West 35th Street, New York, NY 10001

©*1991 David Shotter*
Printed in England by Clays Ltd, St Ives plc

British Library Cataloguing in Publication Data
Shotter, D. C. A. (David Colin Arthur)
Augustus Caesar. - (Lancaster pamphlets)
1. Roman Empire
I. Title II. Series
937.05

Library of Congress Catalog Card Number
91–10053

ISBN 0–415–06048–6

Contents

Appendices

Foreword

Lancaster Pamphlets offer concise and up-to-date accounts of major historical topics, primarily for the help of students preparing for Advanced Level examinations, though they should also be of value to those pursuing introductory courses in universities and other institutions of higher education. Without being all-embracing, their aims are to bring some of the central themes or problems confronting students and teachers into sharper focus than the textbook writer can hope to do; to provide the reader with some of the results of recent research which the textbook may not embody; and to stimulate thought about the whole interpretation of the topic under discussion.

List of figures

Acknowledgements

Thanks are due to Peter Lee of Lancaster University Archaeology Unit for drawing the maps which appear as Figures 1, 2 and 3; Figure 4 is reproduced by permission of Chatto & Windus. Thanks are also due to Mrs June Cross for preparing the original typescript.

Abbreviations

Ann.	Tacitus, *The Annals of Imperial Rome*
BMC	Coins of the Roman Empire in the British Museum
JRS	Journal of Roman Studies
RGDA	Res Gestae Divi Augusti
RIC	The Roman Imperial Coinage

Introduction

History sees Augustus Caesar as the first emperor of Rome, who brought the city and the Empire from the chaos of civil war to a system of ordered government. Of this overall achievement there is no doubt, for Augustus provided a firm and stable basis from which sprang the expansion and prosperity of the next two centuries, and which enabled Rome and the Empire to withstand the waywardness of many of the emperors who came after Augustus.

Augustus' career was not typical in a state which expected its leaders to be both aristocratic and mature in years. His father had risen from relative obscurity to marry a niece of Julius Caesar; on Caesar's assassination in 44 BC, their son, who was one of Caesar's few legitimate male relatives, burst upon the scene at the age of only 18, expecting a supremacy for which most who were socially his betters would have had to wait until the age of 42 or so. Such impetuosity might have proved fatal, but Octavian (as he was then known) displayed a consummate ability to utilise people's services, to play men off against each other, and to maintain a convincing self-righteousness in the most unpromising of situations. Such were the ingredients of charisma in a man who from his earliest years proved himself to be a mature demagogue and a deft manipulator of opinion.

Still more remarkable was the fact that, having achieved supremacy by his defeat of Antony and Cleopatra at Actium in 31 BC, Augustus proceeded to provide the Roman state with a form of permanent governmental supervision. Many had come to see this as necessary, but many, more mature than he, had come to grief in the effort to find an acceptable formula for such supervision. But then Augustus had before him the sternest reminder of the consequences of failure – the assassination of Caesar, his great-uncle and the man who late in life had adopted the young Octavian as his son.

Not only did Augustus institute his own form of permanent supervision of government, but he lived to develop it over a reign of forty-five years and to die in his bed at the advanced age of 77, regarded by most as the saviour of Rome and a man indispensable to its prosperity. He therefore proved equal to a task which many thought impossible; at the same time he managed to project himself as the benevolent patron of all that was best in tradition, despite the fact that in his rise to power in the 40s and 30s BC his behaviour had seemed to many to represent a catalogue of unscrupulousness, crime and opportunism.

How did this remarkable man convince a majority of his benevolence and rectitude? How did he prove to them that he was not 'king' or 'dictator', but *princeps*, the leading citizen amongst equals – and this despite the fact that there were few who did not know how much real power he held? How did he succeed in persuading members of the senate and others to subordinate their wishes and ambitions to his will? What was the reason for the enthusiasm which led people to eulogise Augustus as 'the restorer of the Republic', and sometimes even to want to worship him as a god upon earth? How was it that, after his death, the deified Augustus seemed to live on to become not only an object of general admiration, but also one of emulation for many of his successors?

The answers lie partly in the complexity of the man himself, and partly in the unique nature of the times in which he lived. This study is intended to answer these questions by exploring Augustus' career, by examining the hopes and expectations of his contemporaries, and by understanding what his 'restored Republic' really was, and the means by which it succeeded in satisfying the majority of his fellow citizens.

1

The Roman Republic

The form of government at Rome which we refer to as 'The Republic' was, according to tradition, instituted in 509 BC, and formally came to an end with Augustus' victory over Marc Antony (Marcus Antonius) at the battle of Actium in 31 BC. Because the idea of a Republican restoration has frequently been associated with Augustus' reign, it is necessary to examine the nature of the Republic and what brought it to the point of collapse. We should initially realise that the Roman Republic had nothing necessarily in common with modern forms of government which bear the same name. 'Republic' is derived from two Latin words (sometimes printed as one) – *res publica*; these meant nothing more specific than 'the public concern', and embraced a set of concepts wider than simply political institutions, which together constituted the Roman way of life. The Augustan poet Horace (Quintus Horatius Flaccus) in his so-called 'Roman Odes' (*Odes* III.1–6) showed that the fabric of society, the constitution and role of the family, the practice of traditional religion and a simple sense of morality were all important parts of what made up the *Respublica*.

Naturally, the form of government within the Roman Republic did not remain static during a history of nearly five hundred years; it underwent changes as Rome developed from a small city-state hemmed in by hostile neighbours to the point where by the mid-third century BC she was acknowledged as the 'mistress of Italy' and later still as the head of a large overseas empire. Such changes of circumstance obviously introduced new pressures, new challenges, new people and new opportunities. In general, it is true to say that the eventual collapse of the Republic in the first century BC was due to a failure to adapt the institutions devised for a city-state sufficiently to take account of these new circumstances.

Although the source material for the early Republic is very unsatisfactory, it is fair to say that the government was made up of three elements. The Republic's chief officers (or 'magistrates') were the consuls; two were elected each year and they possessed executive authority (*imperium*). They formulated policy after taking the advice of their aristocratic peers who constituted the senate. Although not bound by this advice, the consuls commonly accepted it and took it to the people (*populus*) in their assemblies (*comitia*) where it was voted into law.

However, this description of the machinery of government does not adequately catch its spirit, for the three elements – consuls, senate and people – were not independent of each other. As we have seen, the aristocracy made up the senate, and it was from its number that each year the candidates for the consulship came; the consuls, once elected, because of their impermanence and because of their own membership of the senate, tended to carry less weight than the collective view of their peers. Further, the popular assemblies which passed the laws were also dominated by the aristocracy. First, voting procedures were arranged in such a way as to give more weight to citizens who were socially and financially superior. Second, a system of patronage operated whereby the rich and influential citizens were patrons in advice and financial assistance to the poorer citizens who were their clients. In this way, in the absence of secret ballots, which were not introduced until the second century BC, the votes of ordinary citizens could effectively be 'bought'.

Thus, the governmental process in the Republic was dominated by the aristocracy, and the senate proved to be the most weighty element in that process. Constitutional theory and governmental practice were in this way widely divergent in the Roman Republic.

Roman society was divided into two groups of citizens – patricians and plebeians. In the early Republic, the patricians alone constituted the aristocracy and enjoyed a monopoly of power – military, political, religious and legal; power was their birthright because only they had the expertise in these important fields. The plebeians were their dependents, relying on them for advice, financial help, and legal and religious assistance. The plebeians,

4

however, constituted a large and varied group of citizens, some of whom had wealth despite their socially inferior status. Rich plebeians were not prepared to miss out on the opportunities that privilege conferred upon patricians, and were instrumental over two centuries (until approximately 300 BC) in waging a campaign that is known as the 'struggle of the orders'.

They were not content with concessions such as the admission by the patricians that there could be a plebeian assembly (*concilium plebis*), presided over by its own officers (the tribunes of the plebs), and able to make decisions over matters affecting plebeians alone. Plebeians who were wealthy enough to finance election campaigns and support themselves in unsalaried offices wanted to be able to enjoy *full* access to power and influence. Thus the 'struggle of the orders' was largely about the opening up of governmental office, membership of the senate, military commands, and state priesthoods to their number. Gradually during the fifth and fourth centuries this was achieved; so too was the campaign to have the decisions of the plebeian assembly and its officers (the tribunes) made binding over the whole population. However, such changes were more apparent than real; the plebeian assembly, like the assemblies of the whole people, was vulnerable in its procedures to those of its members who were wealthy and influential. More important in establishing the character of Roman politics was the fact that the wealthy plebeians who had gained by patrician concessions wanted nothing more than to be accepted by the patricians as part of a 'new aristocracy'. Thus the 'struggle of the orders' did not result in the democratisation of Roman politics, but in a relatively slight widening of the group that exercised power; in practice it was extremely difficult to tell the difference between a patrician and a plebeian aristocrat. Aristocracy or nobility (as the Romans referred to it) was measured by being a member of a family that could look back to forebears who had held the office of consul.

As Rome grew in stature and influence through the fifth and fourth centuries, so naturally the complexity of government grew too. The powers and duties of the consuls were gradually shared between newly-created officers – quaestors, aediles and praetors – each with a particular function to carry out. It became normal for members of the nobility to progress through these offices from the quaestorship upwards to the consulship in what amounted to a career structure for senators (*cursus honorum*). Above the consulship for some was the post of censor, two of whom were elected every five years to hold office for eighteen months, and whose particular functions were the financial assessment of citizens and the regulation of the senate's membership; apart from the censors, all the state's officers were elected for a year at a time.

The Republic did not recognise a distinction between the civilian and military command structures; consuls and praetors commanded armies. This provided the holders of these offices with an additional hold over the ordinary citizens. For, whereas a consul or praetor acting in his civilian capacity was subject to certain legal checks in his dealings with ordinary citizens, as a military commander he enjoyed the power of life and death over his men. This clearly left ordinary citizens less disposed to question the political arrangements of the Republic.

Therefore so long as the senate as a body maintained its hold over the magistrates, its position was largely beyond effective challenge. Civilian and military power were lodged with its members, and they 'toed the line' partly because they were members of the senate and partly because they would need the support of their fellow senators in future election campaigns. In addition, the growing rigidity of the *cursus honorum* was meant to prevent anyone gaining extended periods of individual power or advancing too rapidly up the ladder. Again, although no magistrate was *obliged* to consult the senate, custom and practice dictated that they did, thus allowing the senate to ensure that measures put before the people had its approval.

It should also be remembered that the senate had within its numbers the major priests of the state religious cults. With a population that was always anxious to secure the continuing favour of the gods, the goodwill of the priests was essential. Further, the people were effectively obliged to accept whatever advice these priests/politicians gave them, and so religious manipulation represented a further element of control exercised by senators over Roman citizens. Senators were also considered to enjoy expertise in the administration of justice; citizens enmeshed in the law had little option but to recognise that senators were in effect the only men who could advise and help them through the procedures.

Thus, the hold exerted over the Republic by the senatorial nobility was virtually complete. Their wealth, invested in land, allowed them to control their tenants and make money with which to patronise others – for example, the urban proletariat. Their military, religious and legal expertise led to further means of

6

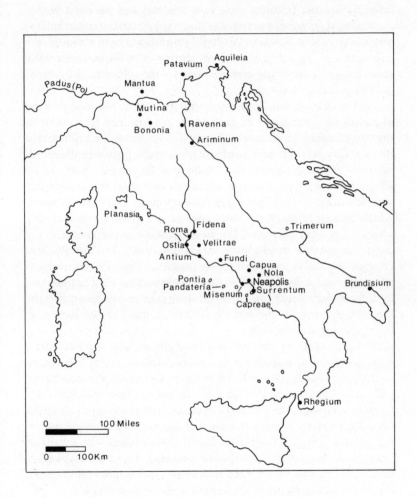

1 Italy

control over ordinary citizens, whilst as magistrates senators were constrained by group loyalty and by the need to remain accepted by their peers. Even the office of tribune of the plebs, which enjoyed the *means* to challenge the senate, was brought under control as the patricians joined forces with rich and influential plebeians in the new nobility; because tribunes were now senators and operated within the senate, they were in practice as much subject to the constraints as other magistrates. It was in fact highly significant that, although the tribunate was not a magistracy, yet it came to be regarded virtually as an integral part of the *cursus honorum* – though open, of course, only to plebeian senators.

The Greek historian, Polybius, writing in the mid-second century BC, admired the stability of the Roman government. In an analysis that owed more to Aristotle than it did to reality he argued that this stability was due to a complex of balancing powers and needs between the magistrates, the senate and the people – or, as he affected to see them, the representatives of monarchy, aristocracy and democracy. Polybius failed to appreciate that the stability, which he rightly perceived, was due not to a governmental theory which originated in Greece, but to the domination of Rome by the senatorial nobility through the means described. To Romans, this prestige and authority of the senate (*auctoritas senatus*) were real and effective – and indeed the more impressive because they required no legal formulae to enshrine them. In short, the senate controlled the government, despite the fact that it had no legal basis whatsoever for exercising this control.

However, just as the senate's strength during the first three centuries of the Republic was its *auctoritas* and its ability to exercise control without legally defined powers, so too, as the conditions and circumstances of Roman politics began from the late-third century to change, the potential weaknesses of the senate's situation began to emerge. As new pressures developed with the growth of the Roman Empire, the senate found that it lacked the means to head off challenges to its corporate *auctoritas*. From the Republic's point of view this was bound to lead to a governmental vacuum; this vacuum was to prove the crisis for the Roman Republic.

2

The crisis of the Republic

Until the mid-third century BC, Rome's influence lay within the relatively narrow confines of Italy; thereafter a series of foreign wars – against Carthage, against the mainland Greeks and against the Hellenistic kingdoms of Asia Minor – transformed the shape of the Roman world and introduced pressures which had never been felt or contemplated in the early Republic, and which gradually highlighted the weakness of a governmental system that relied upon respect for authority and adherence to tradition.

Foreign wars led to the acquisition of territories in which new organisations for government, peace-keeping and exploitation needed to be put in place. The government of the new provinces fell to senators who, as consuls or praetors, had their terms of office effectively extended to enable them after their tenures in Rome to undertake a year as provincial governors; in these extended roles they were termed proconsuls or pro-praetors and could taste a larger and less constrained power than could be exercised in Rome under the watchful eyes of their peers. Inevitably, the sense of ambition to which such power gave rise spilled over into the Republic's domestic politics, and, for the first time, individual senators and the factions into which they formed themselves began to see themselves as more important than the senate's corporate authority.

The new territorial acquisitions gave rise to commercial opportunities which could not be fully exploited by senators; laws restrained a land-owning aristocracy from becoming involved in trade on the ground that it was an activity beneath them. Thus, the chance to exploit the new commercial opportunities fell to others. Some of these were foreigners – mainly Greeks and Jews, who had long been the leaders of commerce in the Mediterranean world. Amongst Romans, however, it was the members of the equestrian order, a group of wealthy citizens outside the senate, who realised that there were fortunes to be made by financing a range of commercial and industrial activities. The equestrian order had previously been a rather disparate body, but now it organised itself into companies of businessmen ready to become involved in commercial ventures. Moreover, because Rome lacked a civil service, these equestrian entrepreneurs were encouraged to spread their interests into activities which might normally be carried out by civil servants – activities such as tax-collection and the operation of the state's industries.

Such involvement brought new wealth and coherence to the equestrian order. Although equestrians generally lacked the desire to become directly involved in politics, they were frequently now the sources of the cash used by senators to patronise and to bribe their way to electoral success. Orthodox wisdom maintained that there was no harm in borrowing heavily to finance election campaigns, since the term of provincial government which followed office in Rome could be used to pillage provincials and thus satisfy creditors in Rome. In this situation the provinces during the later Republic could hardly expect a government distinguished for its fair-mindedness and integrity.

The wealth that flowed into Italy as a result of imperial expansion came in two forms – actual cash and a large pool of prisoners of war who were then sold in the slave markets. Both were considered by traditionalists to be damaging and corrupting in their different ways. The cornerstone of Roman society was the family, which ideally was a self-sufficient unit providing for its own needs. But, for those who could afford them, slaves could be put to work on the land, run the house and educate the children. Such a loosening of the family role was seen as inevitably leading to a declining importance of the family, with serious consequences for the nature of Roman society.

Money could also be invested in land, and slaves were bought to work the consequently larger estates with greater efficiency and thus larger profits. Such estates obviously operated in a financial sense more effectively than small farms whose sole workers were

10

members of the families which owned them. Not only that, but the small farmers found that in the town markets their produce was increasingly in competition with grain that was coming by way of taxation from new provinces like Sicily. Wealth also fuelled building programmes in the towns; these enhanced the reputations of the men who financed them and added to the facilities available in the towns, making them 'magnets' for those small farmers who, out of increasing disillusionment with trying to make a living from agriculture, were flocking to the towns in large numbers.

Urban instability grew in direct proportion to the growth of urban populations, since there was very little work available in the towns for immigrants, who were therefore left little alternative but to survive on the patronage of the rich. However, this shift of population from country to town had another significant consequence. From the early days of the Republic, Rome had not maintained a standing army; rather the ranks of the legions were filled, when the need arose, from the body of Roman citizens who owned property. This amateur arrangement had worked well enough when wars were being fought within the relatively narrow confines of Italy, since the summer season on the whole provided sufficient time for both soldiering and farming. Already, the rigours of more distant campaigns had led to ruin for many small farmers, thus accentuating the drift away from the land. Importantly, as farmers gave up their land, so too they lost their liability for military service. Thus, at a time in the second century BC when Rome's military commitments were growing ever larger, the body of men from which the army could be recruited was growing smaller.

This proved to be the issue over which the relative stability of centuries of political activity broke down. But it is also important not to view the 'military crisis' in isolation, for attempts to relieve it were inextricably intertwined with the efforts of certain aristocratic factions in the senate to outdo their rivals. In the 140s BC a powerful faction headed by Scipio Aemilianus was apparently blocked by its rivals in an attempt to legislate on the issue. A decade later those very rivals came up with proposed legislation which was virtually identical to that which had earlier been rejected. In short, the issue itself was seen by ambitious political factions as less important than the opportunity it offered for building up a power-base. In view of this, it is hardly surprising that the outcome was violent.

Tiberius Gracchus, as tribune of the plebs in 133 BC, attempted to move surplus populations out of the towns (particularly Rome) and

11

back on to the land, and so renew the qualification of such people to serve in the army. He took his proposal straight to the plebeian assembly, as he was legally entitled to do, and ignored the senate. It seems reasonably clear that Gracchus was less concerned with the fates of the urban unemployed and the military recruitment crisis than he was with trying to establish a dominant power-base for himself in the plebeian assembly and trying to remove the senate from the governmental process.

Thereafter, violence was at best only just beneath the surface of the politics of the Roman Republic. Battle-lines had been drawn between two broad factions of the aristocracy; the self-styled *optimates* (or 'best men') believed that the continued supremacy of the senate was essential, whilst their opponents, to whom they gave the title *populares* (or 'mob-panderers'), sought to base their power on the popular assemblies. It should be remembered, however, that both groups consisted of senatorial aristocrats seeking dominance for their factions, and neither had much interest beyond that narrow objective.

The implementation of the Gracchan solution to the problem of army recruitment proved to be of short-term use only; by the last decade of the second century BC the problem was just as severe. On this occasion a more radical solution was proposed by Gaius Marius, who was consul in 107 BC and continuously from 104 to 100 BC. Marius abolished the long-cherished property qualification for military service, which had been thought to be a guarantee of a soldier's loyalty. However, whilst Marius may have solved the recruitment problem by opening up legionary service to all citizens, in so doing he created what has been called the 'vicious nexus' between the armies and their commanders.

The trouble lay partly in the fact that, as we have seen, Rome's military commanders were not professionals, but senators occupying military posts as part of the *cursus honorum*. This had caused few problems whilst the amateur army of farmers relied for their economic well-being on their farms and looked to return to their farms when campaigns were over. Under Marius' new arrangements the army no longer had that basic stability and relied on its commanders to make it wealthy through profitable campaigning and to arrange on return from campaign for the provision of 'discharge payments' in the form of land-grants. The Republic's failure to make automatic provision for these meant that armies and commanders were thrown together into a mutual dependency; because armies required the help and support of their commanders, it was a normal expectation on the part of the commanders that they could utilise their armies' sense of gratitude as a means of furthering their own political ambitions.

On several occasions in the first century BC the Republic found itself blackmailed by its army commanders with the threat of civil war – by Cornelius Sulla in 88 and 82 BC; by Pompey and Crassus in 71 BC; by Pompey, Crassus and Caesar in 60 BC; by Caesar in 49 BC; and by the young Octavian in 43 BC.

The expansion of Empire precipitated other factors, which militated against the stability of earlier days. It was perhaps inevitable that changing attitudes in Rome would be reflected in Rome's relationship with the rest of Italy. Whilst some Italians had been granted Roman citizenship and were therefore enrolled in the citizen assemblies, many more were not so privileged, but had been expected to contribute their menfolk to the allied contingents which fought alongside the legions. Through the second century such soldiers were made to feel increasingly underprivileged and were subject to an increasingly harsh and arbitrary discipline by Roman officials. They came to see that their salvation lay in becoming Roman citizens. Whilst some Roman senators undoubtedly saw the justice of this, many more were worried about the effect on their ability to control what would come from a sudden, large influx of new citizens into the citizen assemblies; such control would be more difficult and more expensive. Decades of frustration for the Italians eventually spilled over into the so-called 'Social War' (91–89 BC), in which Romans fought against Italians, but as a result of which the citizenship concession was grudgingly granted. Nor was there after this any reason why the principle of expanding citizenship should stop at Italy.

Again, the influx of foreigners as a result of the wars led to social and cultural changes, as Greek teachers, poets, historians, philosophers, architects and others came to ply their trades in Rome. The simple Italian traditions came to many to seem very home-spun as the Romans looked for new experiences with which to diversify their lives. But for some the simple traditions which seemed synonymous with the best of the past were seen as being corrupted by the new ideas. In no field was this more obvious than in religion. We have seen that the traditional religious practices provided a powerful means by which the aristocracy in their priestly roles could exercise control over the mass of the citizens.

At the same time it has to be remembered that the cults of gods like Jupiter, Juno and Mars were basically concerned with the well-being and success of the state and were not in any real sense directed to the spiritual needs of individuals. Religious cults of a very different nature, mainly from the east, found their way to Italy as communications in the Empire improved. Most of these were personal religions which stressed a relationship between a god and the individual devotee, and for this reason they attracted interest, particularly as the uncertainties of life seemed to increase. Senators recognised that the growth of these religions would weaken their own hold over ordinary people; for this reason, and also because of the fear that some of these religions might be morally or politically subversive, the senate tried to outlaw them. As early as 186 BC a decree was issued putting severe constraints on the practice of the orgiastic rites of the god Dionysus. The decline in the observance of the old religious practices was yet another sign of a changing world and, together with the decline in the importance of family life, it represented a significant departure from the traditional *pietas* (piety), a virtue implying a simple and respectful attitude towards gods and family.

By the beginning of the first century BC, confidence in the standards which had seemed to represent the spirit of Republican life was severely shaken; in particular, the governmental stability of the early Republic was in tatters as the series of challenges to the senate's *auctoritas* had demonstrated the real weakness of that body. More important now were the individuals and factions who rivalled each other for supremacy. In short, the Roman Republic and its Empire were fast becoming ungovernable.

Although it would be a gross exaggeration to say that there was any kind of consensus about finding a solution, a number of politicians for varying motives showed by their actions that they believed that the only real solution to the problems of the Republic lay in a concept which in traditional terms was deeply distasteful – namely permanent or semi-permanent supervision of the government by an individual. The distaste sprang partly from an old fear of kingship and partly from the practical anxiety that dominance by one man was bound to interfere with the freedom and legitimate ambitions of others. A more cynical view might render these as privileges and vested interests.

In 82 BC, Sulla, having won power in a bloody civil war, used the office of dictator to initiate a number of reforms designed to seat the senate firmly back in the saddle of government; these reforms were repressive both in nature and in their execution. The resentments which they stirred up, and the deep corruption of many of Sulla's henchmen, doomed the reforms from the start; and by resigning in 79 BC Sulla showed that permanent supervision was not part of his scheme. He clearly hoped to carry the necessary reforms to restore respect for the senate's *auctoritas*, and then trust that it would prove stable. In this situation, it was likely that Sulla's laws would be obeyed only by those who wished to obey them, and in 71 BC, Pompey and Crassus used their armies to win the consulship for themselves and as consuls they formally reversed Sulla's work. Popular though this may have been, it did little else than restore the unsatisfactory situation that had existed before Sulla.

The 60s represented a decade of progressively more damaging sniping between supporters and opponents of Pompey whose military prowess elevated him to a dominant position, though he held no office. Perhaps inspired by this idea of dominance without office, and certainly carried forward by an optimism which had no real justification, the politician and orator, Marcus Cicero, became obsessed by the vision of a Roman Republic in which all patriotic men, whether senators, equestrians or ordinary citizens, would fall into line behind a senate that earned and enjoyed respect. At various times Cicero referred to this as the 'union of the orders' or 'union of good men'. Personal ambitions would be set aside, and a man of prestige would guarantee the stability of the senate's position. At various times in his life, Cicero tried to engage the interest of Pompey, Caesar, even the young Octavian, in a scheme which in many respects seems to foreshadow the Augustan principate.

Cicero's hopes of turning his vision into reality soon crumbled before the divisive politics of personal ambition. In 60 BC, the senate, encouraged by the cantankerously traditional Marcus Cato, saw fit to obstruct at one and the same time the needs of the three most powerful men in Rome – Pompey, Caesar and Crassus. Not to be thwarted they joined their political, financial and military resources in the First Triumvirate – an informal arrangement whereby they ordered the government of Rome to suit themselves. Ten years later, with Crassus dead, Caesar and Pompey rivalled each other for supremacy; Pompey's obduracy led to Caesar's armed invasion of Italy in 49 BC, and his own death a year later.

Caesar's control through the dictatorship was more direct and authoritarian than any since Sulla's; he showed the line of his thinking by his observation that Sulla had been a fool to resign his dictatorship when he had put his reforms in place. Caesar had clearly come to believe that the stable operation of the Republic's government required the direct and permanent supervision of one man. However, whilst many might tolerate direct supervision in the short term as a way back to normality, few members of the nobility were truly happy with the long-term direction that Caesar seemed to envisage. Further, the suicide of Cato in 46 BC, because he could not bear to live in Caesar's Republic, proved to many that there was a limit to their compromise of traditional principles and in a sense therefore made Caesar's failure inevitable.

The initial success and ultimate failure of Julius Caesar demonstrated the existence of two problems which continued to beset the Republic – the tendency of armies to support individuals in preference to the senate and people of Rome, and the fact that an acceptable form of supervision of the Republic's government remained elusive. At home Caesar gave an increasing impression of domination, particularly when, early in 44 BC, he became 'perpetual dictator', a move which seemed to deny the Republican principle of regular accountability of its magistrates. His curbing of the privileges of the nobility seemed harsh and abrasive as he filled the magistracies with his nominees and treated the senate as little more than a rubber-stamp.

More positively, Caesar's views on the role and treatment of the Roman Empire were clear and progressive. He believed that imperial expansion should be undertaken with the aim of creating a buffer of territory around Rome and Italy and should aim towards achieving frontiers that were clear and properly defended; for their part the provinces of the Empire should be able to expect fair government and equitable taxation, whilst provincials should be integrated into a world-empire by the expansion of grants of Roman citizenship and thus be given the opportunity to take an important part in their own government. Caesar reformed in all these areas, though a coherent approach to the problems had to wait until the reign of Augustus.

As we saw earlier, *Respublica* was a term which embraced many different ideas and concepts – a method of government, a set of institutions, the ambitions of a particular class within those institutions, and aspects of and attitudes to a traditional way of life. It was all-embracing, yet frustratingly intangible; it is little wonder that Caesar, perhaps out of aggravation at something with which he

16

could not come to grips, dismissed the *Respublica* as a 'mere name without form or substance'. Yet he himself knew the strength of that 'mere name', for it had precipitated him into civil war in 49 BC.

As dictator in the 40s BC, Caesar realised, as many had done before him, that it was essential to prevent this *Respublica* from slipping into anarchy, but he apparently forgot the lesson of the 50s – that it was not sufficient for success to carry a majority of the population with him. In November of 50BC, 370 senators had voted that peace was more important than a war fought over the ambitions of Caesar and Pompey; yet 22 others thought that it was worth embroiling Rome in civil war to make the point that their freedom (*libertas*), which was their self-proclaimed 'right' to enjoy their privileges and enhance their glory, had to triumph over all other considerations. It is proof of the capricious nature of the *Respublica* that this minority was able to have its way, through manipulation of the machinery of government.

If Caesar believed that never again would such bigotry succeed, he was wrong; he was mistaken too if he thought that the trauma of civil war would make people more reasonable and ready for compromise. For some, a major question still existed not just over whether the Republic needed direct institutional supervision or something which lay outside institutions, but over whether there should be any supervision at all. Caesar's insensitivity on this issue led to frustration and failure; as his friend Gaius Matius was to write later, Caesar 'for all his genius could not find a way out'.

Caesar's approach was direct: the destructive urges of the nobles, whether as senators or magistrates, had to be curbed. His well-known kindness and consideration for his enemies did not help, for many saw clemency, which could be removed as easily as it was granted, as a sign that Caesar was the 'master' (*dominus*) who interfered with *libertas*, not a 'first among equals'. Although Cicero's vision of a 'union of good men' did not become a reality in his lifetime, it was, by its emphasis on the *auctoritas* of the senate and of the senior figure who guaranteed stability, more in tune with tradition than the ideas of Caesar the dictator. In short, a solution to the problems of the Republic awaited a hand that was weightier than Cicero's but a good deal more deft than that of Julius Caesar.

3
Octavian

Gaius Octavius, whom the world came to know better as Octavian and later Augustus, was born on 24 September, 63 BC; this was the year of Cicero's consulship and the year in which the great orator came to recognise that the Republic needed reform, if it was to maintain stability. Octavius' father and grandfather both bore the same name as he; his grandfather was an equestrian banker, whilst his father won membership of the senate and rose to the rank of praetor in 61 BC. Although a family new to the politics of Rome, the Octavii, through wealth and local influence, had long enjoyed a high reputation in their home town of Velitrae, some 25 miles south-east of Rome.

During the 60s Octavian's father appears to have been identified with political activities in which Julius Caesar was involved, though he also won praise from Cicero for his fair-mindedness. It is perhaps not surprising therefore that Octavius' political sympathy with Caesar, combined with a generally good reputation, should have pointed him out as a man destined for higher things. Certainly, his marriage to Caesar's niece, Atia, demonstrates the regard for him in Caesar's family. After his praetorship he held a provincial command in Macedonia where he again acquitted himself well; there is little doubt that it was only Octavius' premature death in 58 BC which prevented him standing for (and probably winning) a consulship.

Atia soon remarried, and her son appears to have enjoyed a good and constructive relationship with his stepfather, the noble Lucius

Marcius Philippus, who was consul in 56 BC. He did not, however, lose his special link with his mother's family (the Julii), since his first public appearance (in 52 BC) was to deliver the funeral oration for his grandmother, Caesar's sister, Julia. Although there is no record of what he said, normal practice would suggest that it went beyond a eulogy of Julia's own qualities to embrace the ancestry and achievements of the Julii; it would not be at all surprising if the career of his great-uncle figured prominently in this.

It was in the 40s that Caesar's interest in the young Octavius became clear; although Octavius' mother tried to ensure that her son was not advanced too rapidly, Caesar secured honours for him and gave him posts on his staff by way of an 'apprenticeship'. The avuncular role appears to have become more paternal. The most significant of the honours obtained for Octavius by Caesar was the elevation in 45 BC to the ranks of the patrician aristocracy; the following year Octavius was to accompany Caesar on his projected eastern campaign, along with some of his own friends such as Marcus Vipsanius Agrippa, who was to play a significant part in his life. Caesar's will, which was drawn up in September of 45 BC named Octavius as his son and heir; Gaius Octavius as a result became known as Gaius Julius Caesar Octavianus. Henceforth, the Roman world knew him as 'Caesar', though subsequent generations (for clarity) have called him 'Octavian', a name which allegedly he hated.

Caesar's assassination on the Ides (15th) of March, 44 BC threw into turmoil the plans and feelings of his adoptive son. No less was the turmoil that descended upon the Republic, for Caesar's murderers, led by Marcus Brutus and Cassius, apparently had no plans for the future other than believing that the death of the tyrant would automatically lead to the restoration of the Republic. In practice, this meant little more than that the nobility would be free to resume their self-indulgent pursuit of wealth, honour and glory. Such freedom had little to offer those left on the margins – the equestrians, the people, the legions and the provincials.

The assassination of Caesar, therefore, left a power vacuum in Rome; this was swiftly, though temporarily, filled by Caesar's 'deputy', Marc Antony, the consul of 44 BC. The Republicans, who now came under the vocal leadership of Cicero, soon regretted their failure to assassinate Antony as well. Antony's eventual weakness, however, was due not to the strength of Cicero and the Republicans, but to his own underestimation of Octavian, which left the latter open to the Republicans' attempts to use him against Antony. It is important to remember that the name of the young Caesar was a powerful draw to all those who felt marginalised by the nobility's resumption of its traditional power battles.

Thus, ignored by Antony, Octavian came to Rome in the spring of 44 BC to cultivate Caesar's friends and associates, including Cicero, whose vanity was excited at the thought that the 'divine youth' (as he called him) should sit at his feet as at those of a political mentor. It was in euphoria at this turn of events that Cicero formulated his plan to utilise Octavian to destroy Antony and his associates. For Octavian this attention could not have been better timed; for, still only 18 years of age, he would normally have expected to have to wait more than another twenty years before he was qualified under the terms of the *cursus honorum* to compete for the consulship.

Throughout the autumn of 44 BC Cicero thundered out his series of 'Philippic' Orations against Antony, leaving no part of the consul's public or private life untouched. At the end of the year, Antony's consulship expired, and he went north to take control of the province he had chosen – the north of Italy, which the Romans called *Gallia Cisalpina* and which they recognised as the gateway to Italy proper. However, spurred on by Cicero, the outgoing governor, Decimus Brutus, who had been one of the conspirators against Caesar, refused to quit. Antony besieged him in the town of Mutina, and Cicero now proposed to send north an army to relieve Brutus. Stripped of Cicero's emotive rhetoric this was an army recruited to make war on the legally appointed proconsul of Cisalpine Gaul, Marc Antony; as if to compound the illegality, Cicero further proposed that Hirtius and Pansa, the consuls of 43 BC (who were the regular commanders of this army), should share their command with Octavian, whom Cicero persuaded the senate to promote by excusing him all offices up to and including the praetorship and thus giving him the seniority of an ex-praetor. The *cursus honorum* would not have given Octavian this position until in his late thirties.

Brutus was relieved – but at a cost, for the consuls were both killed in battle, though some suspected that Octavian had had them murdered. Antony personally escaped capture, and again some suspected the intervention of the conniving hand of Octavian. For Cicero and the Republicans, Octavian had now fulfilled his purpose, and they ordered him to hand over the troops which he commanded to Decimus Brutus. Not surprisingly he refused, arguing that he could hardly be expected to co-operate with one of his father's murderers; Octavian's *pietas* (filial duty) had more than a ring of political expediency about it. Instead, Octavian marched his troops on Rome, demanded (and won) the consulship, and then returned north to meet with Antony and with another of Caesar's close collaborators, Marcus Aemilius Lepidus. Together, they agreed to form a second triumvirate; the 'divine youth' had demonstrated that he had more than his share of mortal ambition.

Unlike the essentially private triumvirate of Pompey, Caesar and Crassus in 60 BC, this Second Triumvirate was formally agreed upon and given the legal status to act as the government of Rome and the Empire. But despite its high-sounding purpose – to heal the Republic's afflictions – its real aim was the service of personal and factional ambition. The three members were the joint leaders of the new Caesarian faction, though it was inevitable that sooner or later rivalry would drive them apart; the Caesarian faction required one leader, not three! As Sulla had done in 82 BC, the Three organised a programme of proscriptions to eliminate enemies and to acquire the funds necessary to keep the populace and the army happy.

Cicero was one of the first to pay the ultimate penalty, and no amount of subsequent propaganda could excuse Octavian his part in this treacherous act. A military campaign was then organised to avenge Caesar's murder and to dispose of Marcus Brutus, Cassius and their followers; at the battle of Philippi (in Greece) in 42 BC the Caesarian faction finally completed the avenging of the murder of its late leader – and as a result of its victory found itself in control of sixty legions, or more than a quarter of a million men.

Following Philippi, territorial spheres of interest were carved out by the Three. On the face of things, Antony was the chief beneficiary, in that he took control of the east which had always been regarded as a great reservoir of resources. Octavian received Italy; this had the advantage of being the heart of the Empire, but it was also the place where great disruption and hardship would have to be inflicted in acquiring the land necessary for settling the veteran legionaries whom the Three wished to demobilise. Italy was also harried by the piratical activities of Pompey's son, Sextus, who had established bases in Sicily and was styling himself with characteristic bravado, 'the son of Neptune'. He interfered with Italy's trade, particularly incoming shipments of grain, and provided a refuge for die-hard opponents of the Three.

21

Antony hoped that Octavian would be submerged beneath such problems, but his brother, Lucius Antonius, had been instructed to ferment trouble just in case they were not enough. For Octavian, however, the high-risk position in which he had been put paid great dividends. Not only did he survive the problems, but he was able to turn them to his advantage. He defeated Lucius Antonius in 41 BC and he managed to control Sextus Pompeius, until finally in 36 BC Agrippa's strategy led to the defeat of the 'son of Neptune'. As problems in Italy receded, Octavian was able to make a virtue out of his control of the west, contrasting his defence of the homeland and its values with the corrupt Orientalism to which he argued that Antony was succumbing in his relationship with his Egyptian mistress, Cleopatra.

Octavian's stature grew with success; the armies run by himself and Agrippa achieved successes which could be advertised as crucial to Italy's security, whilst Antony's armies suffered defeat and lost legionary emblems at the hands of the fearsome Parthians, the main eastern enemies of Rome, who already in 53 BC had caused the defeat and death of Crassus. Success for Octavian and Agrippa against Sextus Pompeius led in 39 BC to an agreement whereby those Republicans who had taken refuge with Sextus were allowed to return to Italy. The return of members of some extremely prestigious families allowed Octavian to claim credit for their rehabilitation: importantly they could be used to add distinction to Octavian's Caesarian faction and thus save him from the appearance of regality from which Julius Caesar had suffered because of the absence of such luminaries.

Even more important than this general re-alignment was the marriage between Octavian and one of the most aristocratic young ladies available, Livia Drusilla. The marriage caused a scandal at the time because Livia was already pregnant; yet her husband, Tiberius Claudius Nero, appears to have voiced no objections. Octavian not only gained the social and political prestige which such a marriage was bound to bring him, but he also brought two stepsons into his household – Tiberius (the future emperor) and Nero Drusus. Again events provided material for Octavian's propaganda, for he was able to minimise the scandal which his marriage occasioned by throwing the weight of his invective against Antony's relationship with Cleopatra; he was able to point out not only the inherent undesirability of such a union, but also the fact that its chief victim was Antony's wife and his sister, Octavia. It would not be an exaggeration to say that the marriage to Livia represented one of the most important decisions of Octavian's life.

Octavian, the leader of the Caesarian faction, was now the champion of Republicans and the defender of patriotism, nationalism and traditional respectability; the contrast with the faction of Julius Caesar could not have been greater.

The west was being prepared for a war that was portrayed not for what it really was – a civil war fought between two rivals for political supremacy – but as a great national crusade to defend Rome's integrity against Oriental barbarism and corruption. Italy swore to defend its champion in the forthcoming crusade; 'Italy United' was the battle-cry for the campaign against Antony and Cleopatra.

In 31 BC, at the battle of Actium off the Greek coast, Octavian's armies were victorious, and Octavian had won the civil war. The following year, the deaths of both Antony and Cleopatra left him in undisputed control, with enormous wealth and prestige – the means to control and persuade the Republic. For the new Caesarian faction and the new Caesar, the time had now come to re-order the Republic. The omens for Octavian were far more favourable than they had been for his adoptive father in 49 BC. Octavian had guided Italy through its perils and had saved it in battle. Against a background of almost unanimous support due to the conquering hero, he now had the opportunity to produce a political formula which would allow the Republic to have *libertas*, but yet give it the coherence and protection of a permanent supervision which had long been seen by many as both necessary and inevitable.

4

The powers of Augustus

The battle of Actium has always been viewed as a turning-point in the history of Rome – the end of the Republic and the beginning of a new monarchy. The latter has usually been styled the 'Principate', from the Latin word, *princeps*, which was used to describe a 'leading citizen'. It is, however, important to notice that even after Actium, the word *Respublica* continued to be used of the state, and that well before Actium leading citizens had been referred to as *principes* (the plural of *princeps*). Therefore the terminology in use made no clear distinction between the periods before and after Actium. Further, references on public inscriptions to 'restoration' were clearly intended to stress the Republic's perceived continuity. Despite this, however, generations of scholars have tried to argue the question as to whether or not Augustus can be described as having restored the Republic.

As we have seen, *Respublica* embraced a broad collection of ideas relating to the governmental and social fabric of Rome. It is clear from the brief review of Augustus' reign given in the early second century AD by the historian Tacitus (*Ann.* 1.2; see Appendix III) that that author was in no doubt that in Augustus' time the government of Rome moved markedly towards monarchy. Tacitus' references to *dominatio*, and to the existence of a 'royal family' (*domus regnatrix*), show that he at least recognised the existence of a radical change: 'equality', Tacitus states, 'was a thing of the past and everyone looked to the orders of the *princeps*'. Elsewhere,

Tacitus stressed the incompatibility of the Principate (*principatus*) and *libertas*. Yet, it is hardly conceivable that, had Augustus' offence against *libertas* been as obvious as that of Julius Caesar, he would have survived, let alone come to be widely viewed at the end of his life as indispensable to Rome's stability and prosperity.

The impressions gained through Tacitus' analysis of the period and the fact of Augustus' survival to old age clearly combine to suggest that Augustus' programme was acceptable on the grounds of its gradual nature; in short the career of the *princeps* did not *look* like one of accelerating usurpation.

Octavian's emergence on to the scene in 44–43 BC, although clothed in the respectability of filial duty (*pietas*), precipitated him into a role in which many, if not most, observers found his behaviour outrageous. The 30s, in contrast, were a significant period for the retrieval of this situation; Octavian appeared to become more, not less, respectable. He saved Italy from the piratical maraudings of Sextus Pompeius and welcomed back to Italy the remnants of those families which had detested dictatorship and triumvirate in equal measure; he even married into one of the most respected of these families. He protected the territorial integrity of Italy from the dangers posed by European enemies and, most impressively, he withstood the threat which he argued was posed to Italy's and Rome's traditional values by Antony, once his fellow *triumvir* but now little short of being an Oriental despot. He achieved primacy in the Caesarian faction and, through it, the duty of protecting and promoting the government of Rome; in short, his role as 'restorer' was established.

The task of 'restoring the *Respublica*' had originally been given to the Second Triumvirate in 43 BC, but had been interpreted in different ways by different people. The narrow ideas of nobles such as Brutus and Cassius were balanced in the 30s by Octavian's patronage of new nobles who owed their promotion to him. The attachment to Julius Caesar of the army and the urban *plebs* was readily transferred to Octavian, as Caesar's heir. Nor could anyone deny that the increasing peace and stability within Italy brought with them a range of benefits. In fact, the interests of Octavian himself and of almost every group in Rome saw increasing convergence during the 30s.

The propaganda machine of Octavian had encouraged Romans to view the battle of Actium as the climax of a crusade. It was important to Octavian that the unity which had been achieved in that crusade should not weaken now that victory had been secured; but in reality the task of ensuring a return to normality, which had been the brief of the Second Triumvirate, still had to be accomplished. It was essential therefore that, as leader of the Caesarian faction, Octavian should be able to channel the enthusiasm which he had engendered into the harder task of reconstituting the Republic.

He judged that for a short time after Actium he could allow some of the passions to cool; the consulships which he held each year and the residual powers from the Triumvirate enabled him to govern Rome in the meantime, whilst he basked in the adulation that was focused upon him as the victor of Actium.

The first proper step was formally to end the emergency: 'in my sixth and seventh consulships, after I had extinguished civil wars, and at a time when with universal consent I was in complete control of affairs, I transferred the Republic from my power to the control of the senate and people of Rome' (*RGDA* 34.1, referring to 28–27 BC). The protests at his apparent offer of withdrawal from government were predictable, and they led to a proposal from the senate and people that he should accept a revised role which consisted of a form of institutionalised control. This 'First Settlement of the Principate', as it is known, provided Octavian with two major elements to his control: he would hold a consulship each year, and he would be, for a ten-year period, proconsul of an extended province, comprising Gaul, Spain and Syria.

These powers were derived legally and properly from the senate and people and their holder was formally accountable to these bodies – on an annual basis for his tenure of the consulship, and at the end of the ten years for his tenure of the proconsulship. These powers gave Octavian most of the control that he needed, since Rome could be governed through his consulships, whilst the Empire would be protected by the armed forces which were stationed in his 'extended province'. Indeed these forces represented the bulk of the Roman army, and, although the army was the state's, the soldiers, in accordance with tradition, swore their oath of allegiance through and to the holder of the state's *imperium*, who was their commander (*imperator*). Like Pompey in a similar situation before him, Octavian elected to run his provinces through 'deputies' (*legati*), who were themselves ex-consuls and who were chosen by Octavian for their efficiency and reliability.

The inception of this arrangement was well-timed, for Octavian had maintained a high public profile through 29 and 28 BC. His victories were publicly celebrated, and hand-outs made from the war-booty. He put great effort into the restoration of temples. Above all, the victorious benefactor and guardian of tradition carried out a review of Roman citizens and of the senate's membership; this gave him the opportunity to weed unworthy elements from the senate, replace them and fill the gaps caused by the recent civil war. He created new members of the patriciate, the inner core of the aristocracy, and when the whole task was complete he published a new senatorial list with his own name at its head as 'leader of the senate' (*princeps senatus*, which was a formal title, in contrast to the form of address, *princeps*). This First Settlement of the Principate represented a fairly direct, though not ostensibly offensive, way of exercising control. The state's officers were elected as usual, although Octavian was himself automatically elected to one of the two consulships each year; the rest of the provinces retained their traditional form of government, being controlled by proconsuls, who might be ex-consuls or ex-praetors according to the standing of individual provinces. The senate met to discuss what the consuls and other competent magistrates put before it, and issued its advice to them in the form of decrees (*senatus consulta*), whilst the *populus* and the *plebs* passed laws and elected magistrates.

In outward form at least the *Respublica* was thereby restored, and the Republic's gratitude to Octavian was fulsomely expressed; wreaths of bay-leaves and the civic crown ('for having saved the citizens') were attached to his door, and a golden shield was placed in the senate house awarded, as the citation read, for *virtus* (courage), *clementia* (clemency), *iustitia* (justice) and *pietas* (piety). Most significant was the name Augustus – an honour which linked its owner with the 'august augury' which had accompanied the foundation of Rome, and which was etymologically connected with *auctoritas*. The previously obscure Gaius Octavius had now become Augustus Caesar.

The First Settlement lasted until 23 BC, when a major revision was undertaken. Although the absence of the *princeps* abroad for most of the intervening period avoided a direct impression of domination, yet dissatisfactions and administrative weaknesses appear to have combined to suggest to Augustus that a reappraisal of his position would be timely.

Ill health was probably a factor in Augustus' decision, although tradition has always linked the reappraisal with two other events.

In 24 BC, Marcus Primus, proconsul of Macedonia, a province that was not under the control of the *princeps*, appears, without the senate's orders, to have carried warfare outside his province into the neighbouring kingdom of Thrace; he was condemned for treason. Possibly connected with Primus was an apparent conspiracy the following year involving Fannius Caepio and Murena who was probably the same Murena who was Augustus' consular colleague in 23 BC and brother-in-law of his confidant, Gaius Maecenas. Both Caepio and Murena were put to death, but the full facts were never brought to light. The offence of Marcus Primus seems to have shown that a proconsul with an army could act in a way other than according to the wishes of either the *princeps* or the senate. Augustus' position under the First Settlement afforded him no authority outside his own provinces. Further, amongst the nobility at least, his continuous holding of the consulship will have given pause for thought, since it did not accord with Republican tradition, and partly closed off the office of consul to other aspirants.

Augustus' redefinition of his position in 23 BC is known to us as the 'Second Settlement'; henceforth the pillars of his control were twofold. First, his proconsular *imperium* was changed to make his military authority broader and less specific; it was elevated to become overriding (*maius*). This meant that, instead of being in charge of three named provinces, Augustus was directly in control of all provinces which required a military presence, and the legions were concentrated almost exclusively in those provinces. The other provinces were referred to as 'senatorial' and continued to be governed in the traditional way. However, this division of provinces was made flexible, so that the *princeps* could take control of any provinces that might come to require a military presence and relinquish those that had become pacified. Further, the 'overriding' facet of the *imperium* meant that, when necessary, Augustus could intervene in the administration of any province – even if only temporarily – to counter a threat, or simply, as is shown by the Cyrene Edicts of 7 BC, to ensure good government. As before, all the provinces for which he was directly responsible were administered for him by deputies. This change in effect meant that ultimate military authority throughout the Empire resided with Augustus.

The second pillar of the settlement, and one to which Augustus himself gave a high public profile, was the tribunician power (*tribunicia potestas*); his tenure of this power was henceforth recorded on all public documents, and its annual enumeration used to denote the passing of regnal years. Tacitus described the tribunician power as the most important feature of the powers of the *princeps*. Henceforth, Augustus did not hold the consulship.

Although Augustus had been born a plebeian, he had been enrolled by Julius Caesar amongst the inner core of the aristocracy, the patricians. He therefore could not by definition hold the office of tribune of the plebs. It appears that in 36 BC the plebs had bestowed on Octavian a kind of honorary membership of the college of tribunes; under this, he probably enjoyed the privilege of personal protection, though no specific powers of the office.

In 23 BC, this honorary role was considerably enhanced so that Augustus could employ all the facets of the office. These included the rights to put proposals to the plebs and to consult the senate; as far as government in Rome was concerned these rights compensated for much that he had lost by surrendering his annual tenure of the consulship. Of course, in normal circumstances the tribunes of the plebs were of relatively junior status, ranking below consuls and praetors, who enjoyed the right to consult the senate ahead of tribunes. A special right conferred upon Augustus the privilege of putting his business to the senate before other officers. His tribunician power gave him the use of the tribune's veto, the power of compulsion to obedience, and the power to come to the aid of an 'injured' plebeian. The latter may have been the origin of the emperors' appellate jurisdiction, although it is usually argued that this and primary jurisdiction derived from the proconsular *imperium*.

The powers which went with the *tribunicia potestas* were obviously of great governmental importance and had the virtue of being associated very closely with the traditions of the past; they will also have appeared as a natural confirmation of the patronal authority which Augustus was able to exercise by virtue of his *auctoritas*.

Despite the public emphasis put on the *tribunicia potestas*, there is little doubt that the ultimate sanction of the *princeps* lay in the proconsular *imperium*. The legions were not on public display in Rome, but the 9,000-strong praetorian cohorts, though dispersed into small towns in Rome's vicinity, were a closer reminder of where the real strength of the *princeps* lay. No further constitutional changes followed the Second Settlement, and it remained the basis of government for the next two centuries. Augustus received no further powers, and arguably needed none. He may have had an *honorary* seat near the consuls, but he did not become consul again after 23 BC. Nor did he need to; for the *imperium* which he had as proconsul did not lapse when he entered the city. Although normally the *imperium* of a proconsul could not be used within the city, Augustus did seek and win the permission of the senate and people over the years to employ it for certain specific tasks.

In any case, his *auctoritas* would again no doubt have been sufficient for him to persuade others to carry legislation which he desired to see. A good example of the way in which these various methods could be interwoven is to be seen in Augustus' reforms of the marriage laws: in 18 BC he had himself secured initial reform by means of a bill passed through his tribunician power (*Lex Julia de maritandis ordinibus*); this was supplemented by a law (*Lex Papia – Poppaea*) passed on his behalf in AD 9 through the agency of the consuls, Papius Mutilus and Poppaeus Secundus.

The great flexibility evident in these powers and privileges, as well as Augustus' innate good sense, kept him from accepting further powers of which he had no real need. Because of its unfortunate past associations, he refused a dictatorship; despite pressure in 19 BC, he refused a perpetual consulship; and he avoided taking on an open-ended 'control of laws and customs' (*cura legum morumque*). Only once did he respond positively to the offer of extra powers: in 22 BC, during an acute corn shortage, he accepted a very temporary control of the corn supply (*cura annonae*).

Despite this, Tacitus viewed the remainder of Augustus' prin- cipate as a period of continuing accumulation of domination; this was marked by redefinitions of the status of provinces – whereby his military power was enhanced – the development of a 'civil service' out of the senatorial and equestrian orders, and by the inexorable progress towards the finding of a suitable successor.

Augustus' domination then derived from two sources. A frame- work for government existed in the powers with which he had been invested, and for which he was accountable; the means to make himself the centre of an administrative system had its roots in a concept hallowed by Republican tradition – *auctoritas*. The existence of this provided him with the means to exercise an all-embracing patronage. Writing of this, and referring to the situation after 27 BC, Augustus himself stated:

I excelled all by virtue of my *auctoritas*; of actual powers I possessed no more than my colleagues in the individual magistracies.

(*RGDA* 34.3)

It is a statement of literal accuracy, though the truth of the first part of it could not but render the second part specious in the extreme.

The justification which Augustus put forward for all of this is quoted by Suetonius:

May it be my privilege to establish the *Respublica* in a firm and secure position, and reap from that act the fruit that I desire; but only if I may be called the author of the best possible government, and bear with me the hope when I die that the foundations which I have laid for the *Respublica* will remain unshaken.

(*Life of Augustus* 28.2)

Suetonius' comment too is worth recording: 'And he realised his hope by making every effort to prevent any dissatisfaction with the new regime.'

5

Auctoritas, patronage and the administration

The powers of Augustus, discussed in the previous chapter, have given rise to long and often complex discussions, which have frequently been much concerned with the relationship of these powers with Republican precedent. Augustus himself, however, as we have just seen, clearly regarded these powers as less significant in many ways than his standing or prestige in the state; it was this *auctoritas* that led to the enormous powers of patronage available to him, and it was this patronage that provided the means for the *Respublica* to function.

Auctoritas was in no way a novel concept; in the Republic it had been associated with the senate and had enabled that body effectively to govern the state, despite the facts that sovereignty rested with the *populus* and *plebs* and that the senior magistrates provided the executive branch. Apt comments on the senate's position were made in the third century BC, when King Pyrrhus of Epirus called the body 'an assembly of kings', and later in the first century BC, when Cicero clearly regarded the magistrates as the servants of the senate. Such was the impression given by the senate's corporate *auctoritas* and by that of its individual members.

The senate's discussions (and thus in practice the direction of the *Respublica*) were dominated by its leading figures, the *principes*. These were men who, in or out of office, influenced policy through their prestige, or *auctoritas*; patronage was a measure of that prestige and it is no wonder that Cicero informs us that Pompey was forever

32

boasting of the size and impressiveness of his clientele. The cycle of success/wealth/patronage was firmly anchored in the Republican past.

Thus Cicero, as he tried to formulate a *Respublica* ruled by law and reason, looked to the *auctoritas* of the senate guaranteed by the *auctoritas* of an accepted leading figure, or *princeps*. In the historical setting of many of Cicero's dialogues this was Scipio Aemilianus, the conqueror of Carthage; in contemporary reality, as he hoped, it was Pompey, whom he frequently likened to Aemilianus. A brief study of both of these individuals will lead us to the inescapable conclusion that we should not necessarily expect a *princeps* to be a man of great integrity: Aemilianus' handling of his rivals, Appius Claudius Pulcher and Tiberius Gracchus, and Pompey's handling of his many rivals demonstrate that, then as now, politics was about the survival of the fittest, and that unscrupulous tactics often paid dividends. The positions of both men reflected the esteem that flowed from success.

It is not difficult to cast Augustus in a similar mould: through the 30s he had dominated the propaganda battle with Antony to project himself as a man favoured by gods and the nobility alike and charged with a mission – to preserve the traditional integrity of Rome and Italy. The victory at Actium, and the consequent deaths of Antony and Cleopatra, set the seal on his success. Without doubt or rival he was *the* man of *auctoritas*, who guaranteed the establishment of peace and thus the continuation of the *Respublica*; the unscrupulous, even murderous, behaviour of Octavian the *triumvir* was no barrier to this.

The victor of Actium, however, was not only prestigious; he was wealthy too. Victories brought booty, and to guarantee a continuing source of wealth he succeeded in achieving what in the 60s, 50s and 40s had eluded Pompey, Crassus and Caesar – control of Egypt's immense wealth; the realm of the Ptolemies never became a regular province, but remained the private property of the *princeps* and an important source of his wealth. Augustus' domination through patronage was largely financed by such wealth, although the opportunity to patronise obviously depended upon continuing success.

Augustus could not rest on his laurels; it was necessary both to achieve the right balance in his tenure of powers, and to be ready to modify them as changing circumstances might render appropriate. The combination of dominating and seeming to be the Republic's servant was easy enough to recognise and articulate, but far harder to achieve, as Augustus' successor, Tiberius, was to discover; Dio Cassius, writing in the third century AD, quotes Tiberius as saying on one occasion: 'I am master to the slaves, *imperator* (general) to the soldiers and *princeps* (leading citizen) to the rest' (LVII.8.2). If Augustus needed any reminder of the potential precariousness of the position and role that he held, the memory of the fate of his adoptive father would have supplied it.

As we have seen, the tumultuous final century of the Republic had left a large number of governmental problems to be solved, which derived from the central difficulty of making a government-machine, evolved for the requirements of a small city-state, serve the needs of a large and expanding empire. As Ronald Syme wrote of Caesar:

> His rule began as the triumph of a faction in civil war: he made it his task to transcend faction, and in so doing wrought his own destruction. A champion of the people, he had to curb the people's rights. . . . To rule, he needed the support of the *nobiles*, yet he had to curtail their privileges and repress their dangerous ambitions. In name and function Caesar's office was to set the State in order again.
>
> (*The Roman Revolution*, pp. 51f.)

Whilst such a 'prospectus' might generally apply to Augustus also, there were important differences: as Tacitus observed:

> the most outspoken (potential adversaries) had fallen in civil war or through proscription, whilst the rest of the nobility, the readier they were to play the slave, the more they were elevated with riches and honours, and having profited from the new order of things preferred the safety of the present to the risks of the past.
>
> (*Ann.* I.2.1)

The significant differences between the two situations were the 'curbs', 'curtailment' and 'repression' of which Syme spoke in the case of Caesar, and the inducements which Tacitus implied in the case of Augustus.

Auctoritas, then, and patronage were the means by which compliance was achieved. On the face of things, Augustus' greatest problem lay with the senate and the magistrates, as they would feel first the effects of any slide into open domination – just as they had with Caesar. For the senatorial nobility, the continued

34

importance of the senate itself and of the magistracies, together with their individual ability to climb unhindered up the *cursus honorum*, were crucial; the road of *libertas* led to the achievement of dignity of status (*dignitas*). Caesar's brusque treatment of this whole area had proved fatal. It is of course true that Augustus could expect greater compliance, since he was less troubled by the smouldering resentment of factional enemies than Caesar had been; the transcending of faction, so crucial to Caesar, had to a large degree already been accomplished during the 30s, and the final stages of the struggle with Antony had been made to appear less like a civil war than that between Caesar and Pompey had been.

The senate as a body was in a state of some disarray after Actium; Augustus could therefore, through the revision of the senate carried out in 28 BC, put himself in the role of its benefactor by reconstructing it in a way which found general acceptance but which also ensured that it contained the men he wanted. The *princeps* was also sufficiently strong to leave alone those, like Asinius Pollio, who might not be his natural allies. By restoring the senate's self-respect, Augustus created a body that could work under his patronage. There was no problem, therefore, in using his own consular position or that of others to pass legislation through the senate to the stage of *senatus consultum*. In any case, Augustus assisted the communication of views and ideas between himself and the senate by the establishment, at some time after 27 BC, of a committee, known as the *consilium principis*, where issues could be discussed before any formal approach was made to the full senate. This body, which consisted of himself, the consuls, representatives of other magistracies and fifteen senators chosen by lot, changed its whole membership annually. Together with less formal consultations with leading figures (*amici principis* or the 'friends of the *princeps*'), the *consilium* ensured that the views of the *princeps* were well known to those who would be working with him. Dio Cassius suggests that, although Augustus was a regular attender at meetings of the senate, he was careful not to infringe freedom of discussion by insisting on his view being heard first. It is a clear implication that in Augustus' case, as later in Tiberius', his views, if expressed, would, by virtue of his *auctoritas*, have swamped the freedom of expression of others and thus have damaged *libertas*.

Corporately the senate's standing was greatly enhanced in the process. The senate was also, however, the sum of its individual members, and it was the aspirations of certain of these which had brought them into conflict with Caesar. Although, as we have seen, Augustus' continuous consulships may have created anxiety amongst this group, in general his attitude to the magistracies and those who sought them was much more traditional than Caesar's had been. Until relatively late in his life, Augustus must personally have canvassed for the candidates he favoured, as Tiberius evidently envisaged doing at the beginning of his reign. It was only the onset of old age that led Augustus, from about AD 8, to prefer a more direct way of indicating his favoured candidates, by a method that evidently heralded the later common practice of formal recommendation (*commendatio*). His readiness, however, to leave the procedures apparently open must be taken as an indication of the success which attended his use of traditional canvassing practices.

Success in this represented more than simply persuading the electorate to choose his candidates; for Augustus proceeded to utilise the posts of the *cursus honorum* to provide the beginnings of the senatorial branch of a 'civil service'. Rome had previously lacked a civil service, and had relied on the hazard of the ballot box to produce suitable senators, and (even more riskily) on the financial enterprise of groups of equestrians to collect taxes and manage the state's businesses for profit. Such an inefficient and potentially corrupt arrangement could not be expected to deal effectively with the requirements of a large and complex empire.

Those involved in the senatorial branch of this civil service came to know that although they might be able to trust to their own credentials for electoral success, the backing of the *princeps* would make that success much more likely: it was therefore important to perform the duties of office in such a way as to earn that continued support. The *princeps* kept the performances of the senators in their careers under observation, and on the basis of it made decisions about those best suited to undertake the functions of consul, praetor (legal duties) and quaestor (financial duties), and particularly those who were suitable in terms of efficiency and loyalty to become commanders of legions (*legati legionis*) and provincial governors.

In later periods, because of the much greater body of epigraphic evidence available, the year-by-year operation of such a system of 'promotions' can very clearly be observed. The existence of electoral support from the *princeps*, as well as salaries for the posts themselves, removed the most obvious excuses for the corruption that so disfigured the working of the *cursus honorum* during the Republic. In addition, the monitoring of career performances by the *princeps* helped him in choosing those who should undertake the growing number of curatorships, the creation of which enabled Augustus to control an increasing amount of the administration of Rome and Italy – for example the water supply and the corn supply. This may possibly help to explain Tacitus' comment about Augustus' domination developing through the drawing under his own umbrella of functions that had previously been the preserves of the senate and the magistrates.

Thus Augustus had avoided the abrasive and unacceptable way of dominating the senate and its members that had proved to be the undoing of Caesar. He had in fact found a method more pervasive and more cynical; instead of meeting the nobility in headlong conflict as he curtailed and repressed them, he had brought them under the wing of his patronage and used them and the system of which they were a part whilst appearing to do no more than to uphold the integrity of the Republican system.

Senators, then, almost without noticing it, were brought into the service of the *Respublica*, no longer using the *Respublica* exclusively to fulfil their ambitions. But the senatorial *cursus honorum* represented only a half of the new 'civil service'. A wide variety of state functions had, since the early days of imperial growth, been handled by members of the equestrian order forming themselves into companies (*societates*) to organise such activities as mining and tax collection for profit. At the time, such functions had seemed to develop naturally out of the increased commercial activity which the Empire precipitated and in which senators could not participate. The era of commercial opportunity welded the equestrian order together as never before and made them into a pressure group of consequence.

Despite the fact that equestrian cash was frequently used to finance the election campaigns of senators, a sense of rivalry developed between the two orders, and the animosity involved was frequently the source of conflict. Caesar showed that, with their financial expertise, the members of the equestrian order represented formidable clients. Augustus saw that his political security and administrative efficiency in the Empire offered an opportunity for reform of the order.

The financial and business expertise of the *equites* was recognised; but instead of its being directed towards the ruthless pursuit of personal profit, it was now harnessed to the *Respublica* through the patronage of the *princeps*. The means to achieving this were

37

a complete reorganisation of the equestrian order and subsequent control of its membership through an annual review and the creation of a career structure parallel to that for senators. Just as a lower wealth-qualification of one million *sestertii* was fixed for senators, so a lower sum of 400,000 *sestertii* was introduced for equestrians. A military 'apprenticeship' as a *praefectus* or military tribune preceded a career which included several grades of *procurator*, whose duties covered the running of individual business or financial enterprises, the collection of taxes and, at the top, control of the complete financial arrangements of a province. Such men – as was demonstrated by the infamous case of Catus Decianus in Britain, whose high-handed actions precipitated Boudicca's revolt in AD 60 – enjoyed considerable power exercised independently of the senatorial branch of the service. Above these financial procuratorships came the governorships of certain provinces, followed by a series of powerful prefectures – for example, of the fleet, of the fire brigade, of the corn supply, of the praetorian guard, and, at the pinnacle, of that most important of imperial possessions, Egypt.

Thus, Augustus' patronage of the senatorial and equestrian orders allowed him for the first time to create an imperial civil service which guaranteed efficient management of the Empire. Without it, discontent would certainly have grown in the provinces, requiring a greater expenditure on troops than Augustus wished to contemplate. At the same time, the open and mutual hostility of the orders, which had helped to wreck such dreams as Cicero's union of the orders, was a thing of the past; indeed movement between the orders on financial grounds became accepted, and the emperor could translate equestrians into the senate by providing the necessary subsidy.

Patronage of the ordinary people of Rome was also significant; the *tribunicia potestas* by definition made the *princeps* the patron of the *plebs*, and for a long time he attended and utilised the popular assemblies. But the increasing complexity of governmental processes was bound to demonstrate the increasing unsuitability of the popular masses for participation in them. Gradually, the more direct areas of patronage – 'bread and circuses' – which had helped to create such a bond between Caesar and the Roman people became the central feature of the relationship between *plebs* and *princeps*. Both building work and entertainment were areas of substantial imperial patronage in Augustus' time.

Other areas of imperial patronage (for example, the army and religion) will be dealt with in later chapters, but it would be appropriate to conclude the present chapter with another very traditional and, for Augustus, very effective area of patronage – literature. Just as Aemilianus had patronised the historian Polybius in the second century BC, so now Augustus, through the agency of his friend, the dilettante Gaius Maecenas, organised a group of writers who between them symbolised in their works the aspirations of the Augustan age – Livy, Virgil and Horace. Whilst not the only patron of literature during this period, Augustus may be regarded (by results) as the most successful.

Augustus' patronage in the literary field, as in others, did not force the recipients into a straitjacket. Livy, Horace and Virgil were by no means crude purveyors of Augustan propaganda; rather, their instincts and experience led them to views similar to those of Augustus – that Rome and Italy had suffered inordinately in civil strife, and that peace and a return to traditional values were essential remedies. In the Preface to his *History*, Livy indicates that the depths to which Rome had recently sunk could be offset by a study of the glories of the past; the implication is clearly that such a revelation of ancestral achievements would highlight those figures of the past whose contributions in their own day were of major proportions, and who showed a proper respect for gods, state and family (*pietas*). Further, it is implied that such historical personages could set examples which the modern generation might follow. Livy shared his patron's preoccupation with traditional virtues, and his 'pageant' of seven centuries of Rome's history fulfilled for his contemporaries a purpose similar to that of Augustus' programme of national reconstruction. For public consumption, Augustus shared Livy's preference for a simple patriotism over divisive factionalism.

Similar ground was trodden by Virgil; the practical didacticism of the *Georgics* related well to the policy which Augustus pursued in encouraging the role of the small farmer in Italian agriculture. The *Aeneid* was centred on the Augustan virtue of *pietas*; it was this that moved Aeneas to resist all temptations in his search for a new homeland in Italy. The emphasis on *pietas* was clearly intended by Virgil to throw into high relief a past that should be emulated. The observation, 'How great a task it was to found the Roman race' (*Aeneid* I.33), clearly reflects the enormity of the task that faced Augustus. Aeneas' devotion to his duty (*pietas*) represents the very spirit of the Augustan age.

The *Satires* of Horace, and their exposure of social foibles, were meant as criticism of the unthinking extravagance that represented a departure from the traditional virtues. In the *Odes*, the 'Roman Odes' (III.1-6) present an exposition of these virtues and the importance for Augustus of revitalising them and retrieving the failures of the past. References are made to the programme of temple rebuilding, and to the need to complete Caesar's 'unfinished business' in Britain and to restore Roman pride in the East. Much of the emphasis, however, is on the Augustan return to traditional social values, and the final stanza of III.6 expresses the great urgency of this programme to arrest deterioration: 'Our parents, whose generation was worse than their parents', have brought forth us who are worse still; we shall produce descendants in whom vice is even deeper ingrained.'

Augustus' patronage, therefore, was in this way able to enunciate the problems effectively; by its organisation of government it was able to move towards solutions, though few would have pretended that success was total. It is clear from Tacitus that, even after Augustus' death, some saw motivations for actions that were more cynical than patriotic; it is clear too that some were looking for the return of a *libertas* which the Augustan age had taken away. Equally clearly, however, most were not, as is shown by the remarkable public accolades representing the ultimate seals on the *auctoritas* of the *princeps* – the granting in 2 BC of the title *Pater Patriae* (father of his country) and, in AD 14, the posthumous deification. For many, including his successor Tiberius, who tried to keep alive the Augustan emphasis on traditional virtues, the man that Tiberius commemorated as *Divus Augustus Pater* ('the divine Augustus, my father') was to remain a very strong influence.

6

The *Respublica* of Augustus

We have seen that it was central to Augustus' purpose to base the working of his government on the nobility, both as individuals, and corporately in the senate. On the face of things, the nobles could continue to aspire to enhance their own and their family reputations through the *cursus honorum*: in theory at least it was open to any of them to reach for the *auctoritas* enjoyed by the *princeps*. After all, Augustus himself was to describe one of their number, Marcus Lepidus (the great-nephew of the *triumvir*), as capable of undertaking his burden. It was, however, just as vital that the nobles were taken along with the *princeps* in their corporate (that is, senatorial) function; Caesar had paid the price for his disdainful disregard for that body.

The senate was therefore given a major role in the Augustan Republic. It retained its traditional advisory place in the legislative procedure, and its representatives could influence policy formulation at an early stage through the *consilium principis*. Augustus showed his respect for the senate by his regular attendance at its meetings; in fact, he valued his position as its leading member (*princeps senatus*). However, he could also make laws without its assistance; his letters and instructions to officials, together with the more formal edicts that he issued, all assumed the force of law.

In judicial matters, traditional approaches were integrated with innovations. The old courts (*quaestiones*) continued under the presidency of the praetors to try serious cases involving Roman citizens; but the traditional right of appeal (*provocatio*) which the citizen had enjoyed against the decisions of these and other courts lapsed in favour of a new 'appeal to Caesar'. Since these appeals had in the Republic been rehearsed before the people (meeting in an assembly), the popular participation in the judicial process was thus reduced.

Augustus' most significant judicial innovation, however, lay in the creation of two new courts. One of these consisted of the emperor himself acting in his judicial capacity; the other was the senate exercising a primary jurisdiction. Augustus himself, however, and his successor, Tiberius, made little use of the former. In fact, during these two reigns the senate appears to have gained an important privilege in its ability to try cases brought against its members. However, under some later emperors both courts became instruments of tyranny; Claudius' reign, for example, saw large-scale condemnations of political malcontents (usually senators or equestrians) before the emperor himself. The exercise of the emperor's jurisdiction in this private setting could of course leave defendants completely at the mercy of an emperor and his advisors. The senate's court too was at best a useful addition to the procedures offering defendants a balanced trial before men of experience. Too often, however, under some later emperors, the senate ended up bringing in the decisions which in its fear it hoped the emperor would like to see. In this way, the senate was to become the location of the notorious treason trials under a number of Augustus' successors, when it showed itself incapable of distinguishing between genuine treason offences and what were really trivial insults offered to the *princeps*.

In the financial field also a co-operative system between the *princeps* and the senate was established. The apex of the Republic's finance was the state treasury (*aerarium*), which had since the second century BC been controlled by the senate; it decided on the use made of the Republic's resources, and its officers (*quaestors*) were in charge of the *aerarium*. In the principate, the *aerarium* remained the ultimate source of funds for all the state's activities, including those of the *princeps* himself; control of the *aerarium* was now vested in praetors rather than quaestors, and, since praetors ranked higher in the *cursus honorum*, this change helped to ensure that the officials in charge of the *aerarium* would be acceptable to the *princeps*. Each province had a treasury (*fiscus*), which was not so much a deposit of cash as a statement of income and outgoings relating to each province; these accounts were supplemented, where necessary, with grants from the *aerarium*. The operation and viability of the whole system was, however, clouded by the fact that Augustus frequently subsidised the *aerarium* out of his own resources. Later in his reign, in AD 6, the *princeps* was responsible for the establishment of a military treasury (*aerarium militare*) to cope with discharge payments to soldiers. This function had previously been undertaken by Augustus himself on a semi-private basis, but was now funded through the *aerarium militare* by the proceeds of the sales tax, levied at 1 per cent, and death-duties, levied at 5 per cent.

Responsibility for the coinage was notionally divided between the *princeps* and the senate, with the *princeps* taking charge of gold and silver which was required for the pay of his armies; the senate nominally retained a control of the copper and bronze coinage – that is, the 'small change' in the money system – which was advertised through the appearance on the reverse side of such coins of the letters 'S.C.', or *senatus consulto* ('by decree of the senate'). None the less, all denominations of coinage were used equally for the propagation of information concerning the success and prosperity of Rome and the Empire. For example, coins advertised the capture of Egypt, the recovery from the Parthians of legionary emblems lost by Crassus and Antony, and the promotion of Gaius and Lucius Caesar as 'leaders of youth'.

It is clear from Horace's 'Roman Odes' that the gap between current practices in society and ancestral custom was great and urgently required Augustus' attention for the revitalising of the moral, social and religious fabric of Republican Rome. It was obvious that the last century had represented an escalating departure from traditional standards; luxury, debt, obsession with money and the means of making it were the preoccupations of Horace's *Satires*. Horace virtually imposed a duty on Augustus to stop the rot and instil a new love of the old values.

Rome had of course moved a long way from the simple self-sufficiency enjoined by Cato the censor in the second century BC as the prescription for the ideal Roman. The benefits of imperial growth had been felt by all in varying measure and could hardly be legislated out of existence – although that is precisely what Cato and his friends had tried to do. A century later, many optimate nobles, including the Younger Cato (Caesar's opponent), were verbally espousing a similar cause, though the evidence provided in Cicero's *Letters* shows that they too were thoroughly obsessed by the current preoccupation with wealth and the status symbols which it purchased. In fact, such nobles were little better than those profligate contemporaries on whom they poured a criticism that was deserved but often hypocritically self-righteous in origin.

It was probably a reflection of Augustus' own relatively obscure Italian origins that his own views on such matters were less sophisticated than those of some of his contemporaries; he recognised that excess would have to be pruned away if the 'sense of mission' was to be restored, and that a programme of revitalisation would provide the opportunity for carrying 'Italy United' into action. In other words, he saw it as part of the manifesto on which he had risen to power to reverse certain unwelcome trends in society and thus restore a sense of national unity and identity. Essentially, such simple patriotism was conservative in nature, and later emperors such as Claudius undoubtedly saw the Augustan revitalisation, with its emphasis on Rome and Italy, as far too narrowly based. Yet it suited the contemporary circumstances well. Augustus was no narrow-minded bigot; he did not wish, like Cato the censor, to abolish wealth and all that it entailed. Rather, he recognised that, while Rome was now the centre of a large and prosperous empire, prosperity should not be allowed to undermine traditional values; indeed, it was a central theme of his reconstruction that these values had been building-blocks of the prosperity, and that their retention would lead to even greater success and stability.

All Italy was now to be involved in the changes. Since Roman citizenship by Augustus' time embraced the whole of Italy, and since Rome and Italy together were seen as 'the homeland', it was natural that Augustus should attempt to raise the status and prosperity of Italians. The foundation of new towns (*coloniae*) was a traditional way of bringing unity to territory distant from the city of Rome. Augustus accelerated this kind of activity as he recognised that the resulting unity and stability were essential ingredients in the process of raising the wealth and status of Italians, which were the prerequisites of their taking an increasing role in the administration of the Empire. This role ranged from providing the main source of recruitment to the legions and praetorian guard to entering the equestrian and senatorial orders with their opportunities for senior administrative positions.

The revitalising of Italian agriculture was an integral part of the process of gaining stability and of wealth creation. It also had the great advantage of reminding Romans and Italians of their origins and traditions; it went hand in hand with the emphasis that was also to be placed on the family in the Augustan *Respublica*. The success of Augustus in the integration of Rome and Italy is confirmed in the objections raised later to the emperor Claudius' far more ambitious programme of social reform in the Empire at large; for this was seen by some as destructive of the role of Rome and Italy, which by that time was recognised as central. Whilst Augustus wished to enhance the status of Italy, instinct perhaps, as well as a pragmatism that arose from his dealings with the nobility and their sensitivity over what Caesar had allegedly planned to do, led him to avoid changes in the citizen-body that would have been seen as too radical at the time. In particular, he tried to limit the speed of absorption of non-Italians as citizens through the process of manumission (or freeing of slaves). Restrictions were placed on the status that could be achieved by freed slaves, who under the terms of a *Lex Junia* (17 BC), a *Lex Fufia-Caninia* (2 BC) and a *Lex Aelia-Sentia* (AD 4) were given the intermediate 'Latin' status which prevented them from achieving full social, financial and political rights, though such restrictions did not apply to the children of these freedmen. Many freedmen had carried out duties of a secretarial nature whilst slaves, and continued to do this when freed. Under the emperor Claudius, the freedmen (*liberti*) of the *princeps* became very rich, very influential and bitterly resented. Though Augustus was clearly the ultimate author of such legislation, it should be noted that all the relevant laws carried the names of their individual proposers, indicating the close agreement of the *princeps* and the nobility over this issue.

Augustus himself, however, instigated much of the legislation concerned with the status of the family in society; it was designed to promote regular marriage and child-bearing within marriage. Harsh moves against adultery were combined in different laws (*Lex Julia de adulteriis coercendis* and *Lex Julia de maritandis ordinibus* of 18 BC) with greater freedom of marriage between different social groups. Penalties initially imposed on the childless were gradually replaced by a system of incentives for those with children within regular marriage, so that a man could seek office a year early in respect of each legitimate child.

The success of such measures is difficult to gauge, though Augustus was forced to act upon the laws in the case of his own wayward daughter, Julia, in 2 BC: she was banished and her chief adulterer, Iullus Antonius, was put to death. At any rate such laws indicated that the lax behaviour that had become regular in the late Republic was now an object of official criticism, and the model projected was one that had its roots in earlier attitudes.

Horace was as insistent on the need for religious revival, and here Augustus was offered a major means of manipulation. Observance of traditional practices had long been under threat; as long ago as 186 BC the senate had acted against the wild orgies associated with the imported cult of Dionysus. Roman religion was designed primarily to look to the interests of the state rather than to those of its individual members. Thus, whilst it was seen as being of particular relevance when the state was under threat, it was a different matter in peacetime, and people saw little relevance in the traditional practices. There was an increasing tendency on the part of the literate members of society to turn to philosophy as the best arena for discussion of the spiritual. Ordinary people, to whom this outlet was of course denied, turned their attention to foreign (particularly eastern) religions, the main feature of which was an emphasis on the personal relationship between the individual devotee and the divinity who guaranteed care and salvation.

This trend caused anxiety amongst the governing class in Rome; the foreign influences in themselves were often seen as subversive, whilst the orgiastic rites often associated with such cults were seen as promoting a loose morality. Importantly also, the practices associated with the official religions represented an important part of the hold exerted by the nobility through the priesthoods on the mass of the population. The traditional gods were associated in the minds of the nobility too with a structured order of society that they had supposed prevailed in earlier (and better) days.

There were many ways in which a religious revival was closely related to Augustus' political reforms. It may be assumed that many, tacitly at least, agreed with Augustus when he set out to equate the success of the old days with the protection sought in a traditional fashion from the old gods. *Pietas* ensured the continuance of divine protection, and thus the continuance of prosperity and well-being; many believed (or affected to believe) that the disasters of the recent past were due to the gods' anger at the neglect they had faced. The revitalisation of traditional religious practice was therefore as significant a part of Augustus' programme as the emphasis on old-fashioned family values; both belonged to a time when gods and men were thought to have operated in perfect harmony. Religious revival was a necessary part of the Augustan *Respublica* if this was successfully to claim a close relationship with the old *Respublica*.

Augustus paid great attention to religious detail; temples were restored, priesthoods revived, and he himself took on the role of religious 'chairman' with his assumption of the post of chief priest (*pontifex maximus*) in 12 BC, after the death of Lepidus, the previous incumbent. The climax of religious revival was seen in the celebration in 17 BC of the secular games, sacred to Apollo and Diana. Augustus' own emphasis on the importance to him of Apollo's protection will have served again to stress the connection between himself and the traditional gods and therefore to lend credibility to the restored order of the past. In keeping with the importance attached to family life, he paid particular attention to the household deities, the *Lares* and *Penates*, and to the cult of the hearth-goddess, Vesta. In all, this provided a good example of how religious practices could be put to the service of national policy considerations.

To many, Augustus, for his achievements, was a god on earth; only a supra-human being could have brought stability out of chaos. Not surprisingly, therefore, Augustus found himself the object of acclamations of divinity. However, Augustus might have been a man of *pietas*, but he certainly did not wish to be seen as a god on earth; the acceptance of such an acclamation would have undone his carefully worked relationship as *princeps* with the nobility. Yet it would have been cavalier to snuff out the political enthusiasm expressed through the medium of religion.

The desire to worship the living ruler was tempered therefore; the so-called 'imperial cult' came to be the worship of *Roma*, and only incidentally of Augustus, who protected her. This subsidiary role was present also in the notion of the *genius Augusti*, the guardian-spirit which was held to attend the head of the national family as it attended the head of the domestic family. The imperial cult came to be a focus of loyal attention in the provinces and provided an opportunity for local leaders to project their loyal images. In Rome, it was associated with peace, concord and stability; it was the ultimate expression of *pietas*, and thus of Augustus' guidance of Rome back to its old and hallowed standards.

The *Respublica* was therefore restored, and the Roman state was seen to prosper through the recognition and acceptance of its old standards. Augustus was formally deified on 17 September, AD 14; but, for many, long before that date, he was the almost divine restorer upon whom the security of the whole edifice ultimately depended. We should remember this achievement before being tempted to dismiss his 'restored Republic' as a hollow sham.

7

The Empire and the Augustan peace

Virgil provided what was virtually a 'prospectus' for the Augustan Empire – 'to be merciful to those who submit and to vanquish proud opponents' (*Aeneid* VI.853). Certainly, Augustus' policy was concerned both to secure peace behind firm frontiers and to enhance the prosperity of provinces, once within the Empire. In this way, his work represented a continuation and development of the work of Julius Caesar; this had sought the protection of Rome and Italy by the establishment of a 'buffer' of provinces and pro-Roman territory, secure within visible frontiers and valuing the prosperity which came from peace and security. Such an aim was not born of altruism: it represented the greatest security for Rome and Italy and would bring about major contributions by provinces to their own government – and consequently a manageable burden of expenditure on Rome's part.

Ultimately, the army was the key to the Empire's security, just as it was the key to internal politics. Under the Republic, recruitment and the service conditions of a non-permanent army had led to the close intertwining of the interests of generals and their armies; the consequence was that the Republic suffered from the threat that senators as army commanders could pose to the established order. It was clear that for stability to be re-established the role of the army and its relationship with its generals would have to undergo change.

To a degree, the emergence of a centralised authority born of military power provided a *de facto* solution; first Caesar and then

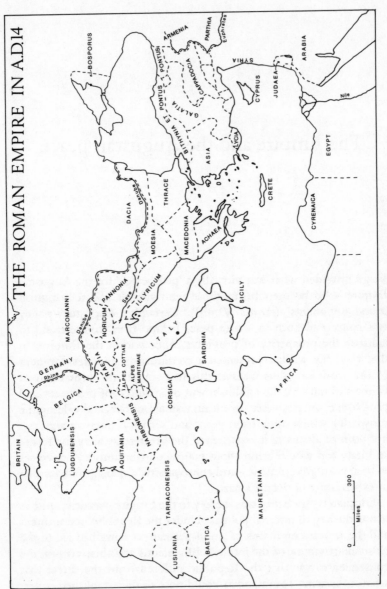

THE ROMAN EMPIRE IN A.D.14

2 The Roman Empire in AD 14

Augustus came to power as a result of military victories won for them by troops who were loyal to them and recognised their *auctoritas* as 'general' (*imperator*) – the military leader with powers of patronage. In 36 BC, Lepidus' attempt to hold Sicily after the defeat of Sextus Pompeius fell apart when Octavian presented himself to the troops as 'Caesar'. The period of the triumvirate achieved much for Octavian in the realm of military stability; during the 30s, following his programme of resettlement after Philippi, Octavian's share of the triumviral armies was used to enhance the security of Italy, and, although the troops were often under the actual leadership of supporters of Octavian, they none the less looked to him ultimately as their general and thus benefactor. At this stage, although soldiers were often in service for long periods, the principle of recruiting for a campaign followed by demobilisation, which was part of Marius' reforms, still applied.

Actium left Octavian with fifty legions under arms; there was no way in which a force of this size could be considered politically safe or desirable or economically supportable. At the same time, Octavian was now in a position to re-organise the Roman armed forces more thoroughly. The aim of the re-organisation was to provide an army that was permanent, professional and stable. The legionary force was reduced to twenty-eight numbered units with a fixed term of service – at first sixteen years, but raised to twenty in AD 6 – and kept up to strength by regular recruitment. Pay was fixed from AD 5 at 225 *denarii* per year, with a bounty of 3,000 *denarii* on discharge. Until the establishment of the military treasury in AD 6, discharges in money or land were provided by Augustus himself, an expensive but sure way of binding the legions to himself. The size of this burden is itself an indication of the level of wealth which Augustus had at his disposal to finance his patronage.

The legions were based in the militarily sensitive provinces, which meant that effectively, because of the proconsular *imperium* which he held as part of the First and Second Settlements, Augustus was their commander, although operating through senatorial officers (*legati*) of his own choosing. After the establishment of the *aerarium militare* in AD 6, the financing of the army was managed from that 'purse' which was kept in funds through taxation. Almost by definition the Roman legions were becoming a frontier-army, and assuming the shape and disposition familiar under Augustus' successors. The legionary groups developed an *esprit de corps* of their own, with an intense pride centring on their emblems and individual numbers. Indeed, the Augustan enumeration was extremely resilient; only legions XVII, XVIII and XIX, which were wiped out in the German disaster of AD 9 and thus considered ill-omened numbers, failed to survive in the legionary list. Recruitment for the western legions and for the Praetorian Guard was basically from Italy and the *coloniae* and *municipia* (citizen-towns) of the west; the eastern legions were recruited predominantly from the east. It is evident that, whilst legionary recruits were supposed to be Roman citizens, many of them, particularly in the east, must have been granted their citizenship simultaneously with their recruitment.

During the Republic a large number of other troops had fought alongside the legions. Originally the Italian allies (*socii*) had made up the bulk of these, but since by the late Republic Italians were included in the body of Roman citizens, this alternative element in the army came to be supplied mostly by kingdoms and cities which had a clientage dependency on Roman politicians. Both Pompey and Caesar had boasted considerable numbers of troops of this sort in the civil war, and they provided the variety that was an essential part of the Roman army.

Augustus organised these kinds of troops into auxiliary units (*auxilia*), which consisted of infantry or cavalry groups of 500 or 1,000 men each. These were commanded sometimes by their own local leaders, but more usually by equestrian prefects or tribunes. These non-citizens were based with and fought alongside the legions, served for twenty-five years, and received Roman citizenship on their discharge.

Besides the field army, Augustus organised the fleet into two squadrons, at Ravenna and the Bay of Naples. For Rome and Italy there were the 9,000 praetorians, who were regarded as an elite imperial guard and were paid three times as much as legionaries, and the less well-paid three units of urban guards. These two groups between them could be regarded as the forces reserved for the defence of Rome and Italy, though occasionally they served further afield with the legions.

Although Augustus appeared to have control over the bulk of these troops through his *imperium* and through the oath that the troops swore to him at the beginning of each year, events were to show that that loyalty still had to be earned; the closing months of Nero's reign demonstrated very clearly that an emperor who was considered not to merit his army's loyalty, might forfeit it. Most emperors took care, as did Augustus, to ensure that the army felt the benefits of their patronage, because they knew that in the final analysis the Principate represented an institutionalising of the 'vicious nexus' between armies and commanders that had broken the Republic. Augustus took care to ensure that his military backing was not overt, but he fully appreciated its reality and significance.

The army might be the ultimate political sanction; more immediately it was the means to winning security and stability in the Empire. In his handling of Gaul, Julius Caesar had demonstrated that he realised the need to adopt a clearer policy on the purpose and extent of imperial expansion. Augustus' policy represented the logical development of this, and an almost constant backcloth to his Principate was provided by the activities of his armies in winning the territory that the new thinking demanded and in consolidating the territory already annexed (see Appendix II).

In Europe, the goal of Augustan policy was the use of the Danube and Elbe rivers as frontiers separating Romans from barbarians; events, however, were to put the Elbe beyond reach, and in the end the Rhine had to be used as the frontier. West and south of these frontiers, a combination of military activity and political initiatives was required to win and then organise territory into provinces.

In the west, Spain was divided into three provinces – Baetica, Lusitania and, in the north, Tarraconensis. Both Augustus himself and Agrippa took part in various phases of these campaigns in Tarraconensis in 26–24 BC and again in 19 BC. Settlement was eventually based on a programme of urbanisation and bringing the native population from the mountainous to the lower regions of the province; settlements of legionary veterans (*coloniae*) were established at places such as Saragossa and Merida, and 'native' towns, like Braga, were founded. The Romanisation of Spain brought great dividends, as it facilitated the exploitation of mineral resources, such as copper and tin, and provided a major source of grain and oil.

In Gaul, Narbonensis, the original province which had been brought into the Empire in the second century BC, and which now required no military presence, was handed over to the senate to govern as one of its provinces. The larger area of Gaul had been embraced in Caesar's conquests (58–51 BC) but still required some pacification, in which Augustus himself took part. This was organised into three provinces – Aquitania, Lugdunensis and Belgica; Lyons took on the role of the administrative and

CHAUCI

FRISII

Vetera

Novaesium

Bonna

Moguntiacum

Rhine

BELGICA

TREVERI CHERUSCI

Argentorate

Danube

LUGDUNENSIS

Vindonissa

Rhône

Augusta
Praetoria

Lugdunum

Vienna

AQUITANIA

NARBONENSIS

Vasio

ASTURES CANTABRI

Arelate

Nemausus

Forum
Julii

TARRAC ONENSIS

Narbo

Massilia

Douro

LUSITANIA

Tagus

Tarraco

Balearic Is.

Emerita

BAETICA

Nova Carthago

Carthage

MAURI

AFRICA

Cercina

MAURETANIA

MUSULAMII

GARAMANTES

0 — 300 Miles

0 — 300 Km

3 The western provinces

commercial centre for the 'Three Gauls', as they were called, and in 12 BC this role was formalised by the establishment there of the 'Altar of Rome and Augustus', the imperial-cult centre for the whole of Gaul. Although the Gallic provinces remained generally peaceful, the legions that were stationed along the Rhine looked to the defence of Gaul should this prove necessary.

For the whole of Augustus' reign, Britain was left outside the Empire, although the *princeps* undoubtedly had some kind of treaty with Cunobelinus, the most influential of the British rulers. Other British chieftains appeared as suppliants in Rome. The mention of Britain by the poet Horace (*Odes* III.5.3) serves to emphasise that Augustus kept a watchful eye and undoubtedly would have seriously contemplated invasion if his diplomatic initiatives in the area had proved unsuccessful. Essentially, however, Augustus did not wish to stretch his military resources by undertaking major activities in Britain, particularly if his objective of non-interference in Europe by British leaders could be achieved by other means.

The rivers Rhine, Elbe and Danube provided the main area of military focus for most of Augustus' reign. The protection of Italy demanded the pushing northwards of Roman territory as far as the Danube, and this process had begun in the 30s BC in the Alpine region; eventually two provinces, Raetia and Noricum, covered the western Danube, whilst the Alps themselves came partly within the small province of Alpes Maritimae and partly within the client-kingdom of Julius Cottius (Cottian Alps). A key feature of the defence of Italy was the establishment of a *colonia* at Aosta. This securing of western Europe was commemorated with the setting up of a great victory monument (*tropaeum augusti*) at La Turbie in Monaco, which detailed the victories won by Augustus' armies.

Western Europe was effectively secure by approximately 15 BC, and attention could be turned to the problems associated with winning and defending clear frontier-lines. Whilst territory south of the Danube had been won in the western region, much needed to be done in south-eastern Europe, where before Augustus' time the only Roman province, apart from the Greek provinces of Macedonia and Achaea, was Illyricum (the coastal area of Yugoslavia) which was renamed Dalmatia. Campaigning lasted intermittently through almost the whole of Augustus' reign and involved both Agrippa and, after him, Augustus' stepson, Tiberius. An initial settlement, reached in 9 BC, was not, however, finally consolidated until after

Tiberius' defeat of the great Pannonian rebellion (AD 6–9). This resulted in the formation of the provinces of Pannonia and Moesia which bordered the Danube from Noricum right down to the river mouth on the Black Sea. In the Balkans, Thrace alone was left under local rulers who, as clients of Rome and Augustus, kept the kingdom loyal to Rome despite the fact that it was left outside the regular provincial organisation.

Augustus was probably happy enough to hold on to the Rhine frontier when so much else was disturbed, but, in 12 BC, he ordered an eastward advance to the Elbe under his stepson Nero Drusus; the objective was to secure the difficult area in the proximity of the head-waters of the Rhine and the Danube (*Agri Decumates* – Tithe Lands). Undoubtedly the enterprise suffered at least a loss of momentum with the death of Nero Drusus in 9 BC. Tiberius, his replacement, had scarcely picked up the threads of his brother's work when his closer involvement in dynastic politics led to his withdrawal to Rhodes in 6 BC (see below, p. 75). Spasmodic activity continued over the next ten years until Tiberius, after his return from Rhodes, renewed what was intended to be the decisive offensive against the tribe of the Marcomanni of Bohemia. It was in the midst of this, however, that Tiberius was called away to deal with the Pannonian revolt.

Although there was a tendency to think of the area between the Rhine and the Elbe as effectively conquered, it would be more accurate to say that it had been traversed by Roman armies; little by way of Romanisation had occurred and some of the tribes, particularly the Cherusci under their chieftain, Arminius, were hardly pacified. The extent of the superficiality of the 'conquest' was made obvious on the arrival in AD 9 of Quinctilius Varus as commander in Germany; he probably owed his appointment to the fact that he had married into the family of the *princeps*, and he proceeded to demonstrate by his introduction of new taxation methods that he had underestimated the complexity of his new job. The result was the ambush and annihilation by Arminius and the Cherusci of three complete legions (XVII, XVIII and XIX). Recent research has put the scene of this disaster in the vicinity of Osnabrück where a considerable amount of Roman military equipment has been uncovered.

Although the disaster was prevented from becoming a total catastrophe by the arrival of Tiberius, fresh from quelling the Pannonian mutiny, it finally closed the door on the dream of a Roman province extending to the Elbe. The disaster had a debilitating effect upon Augustus himself, who is said by Suetonius to have given himself to banging his head against a door, crying out: 'Quinctilius Varus, give me back my legions.' The legionary numbers were never replaced, and Augustus appears to have revised his policy to one of keeping the Empire within its existing borders – a decision which clearly owed more to the trauma of the disaster than, as some alleged, to Augustus' jealous guarding of his own reputation as a conqueror. From this point the Rhine corridor was organised into two military districts – Lower Germany (the northern district), with legionary bases at Xanten, Neuss and Bonn, and Upper Germany (the southern district), with bases at Mainz, Strassburg and Windisch.

Rome's relations with the kingdoms of Asia Minor had developed from her increasing contacts with the Greeks in the second century BC. Many rulers of such kingdoms had over the years chosen to strengthen themselves locally by entering into treaties with Rome, though occasionally some of these 'Hellenistic kings' had tried to resist Rome's progress in the area. The most dangerous of these had been Mithridates of Pontus, who saw it as his mission not only to keep Rome out of Asia Minor but to drive her from Greece also. His determination sprang partly from Rome's bad record of provincial governors and financiers.

Pompey's final defeat of Mithridates in 63 BC was an important milestone; not only did it provide the opportunity for the political settlement of the area but it had also been achieved by drawing into the arena the King of Parthia, inevitably perhaps in view of Mithridates' attempts to strengthen his own hand by alliance with Parthia's neighbour, Armenia. Pompey's political settlement involved three provinces, Asia, Bithynia/Pontus and Cilicia, and a collection of client-kingdoms in the interior of Asia Minor; Roman interests were thus brought up to the borders of Armenia and the Parthians. The risks involved in this were made clear with the defeats at Parthian hands of Crassus in 53 BC and Antony's general, Decidius Saxa, in 36 BC, both of which involved the loss of legionary emblems. For the sake of Rome's pride, Augustus had an obligation to recover these, and his moves to achieve this provided an opportunity to produce a settlement which was more stable than Pompey's.

With regard to the legionary emblems, a much publicised success was achieved in 20 BC by a joint diplomatic initiative conducted by

Augustus and Tiberius, which was itself facilitated by the confused state of Armenian politics. A pro-Roman client-king (Tigranes) was installed on the Armenian throne and the King of Parthia (Phraates) induced to accept a Roman presence in the area. There was obvious merit in the arrangement – good relations between Rome and Parthia, leading to the installation of a king of Armenia acceptable to both parties. Unfortunately such arrangements had validity only so long as the original participants remained. The removal by death (or other means) of the ruler of Armenia or Parthia almost inevitably led to renewed instability.

Augustus tried to strengthen the whole arrangement by re-organising into a new province, called Galatia, much of the territory of central Asia Minor which had previously been left in the hands of well-disposed local rulers. He also made it clear that Syria, the chief imperial province in the area, was one of the most significant in the entire Empire. However, the instability in relations with Armenia and Parthia was endemic, and although the difficulties caused by the deaths of Tigranes and Phraates were temporarily alleviated in AD 1 by Gaius Caesar, the adopted son of Augustus, the area was still in a highly unstable state when Tiberius became emperor in AD 14. He produced a fresh settlement through his nephew, adopted son and heir, Germanicus Caesar, though problems continued to recur in the area throughout the first and second centuries AD.

Roman pride, therefore, had been salvaged, but the eastern part of the Empire had not been left securely settled. To the south of Syria lay Judaea, and here again an area which it had been hoped could be left under pro-Roman local control proved unstable. It was Augustus' policy to avoid antagonising Jewish sensibilities, but the constant conflicts between Judaea's political and religious leaders led to its being organised as a province in AD 6.

In North Africa, the desert formed a relatively effective southern frontier to the Empire. Egypt was, as we have seen, after Cleopatra's suicide, taken as a private possession of the *princeps*; he could use its wealth for patronage and its grain gave him the means to forge a special relationship with the Roman people. In view of Egypt's wealth, the choice of prefect was a particularly sensitive one, nevertheless, at least one holder of the post – Cornelius Gallus – seems not to have resisted the temptations of his office.

The remainder of the North African coastal strip was divided between two provinces – Cyrene (administered with Crete) and

Africa itself, both senatorial – and the client-kingdom of Mauretania. Africa was centred on the now restored city of Carthage, and both it and Cyrene were of major agricultural importance as suppliers of grain. Their chief difficulties lay in the activities of nomadic tribesmen to the south – the descendants of Jugurtha – who during Tiberius' time were to pose a considerable problem under the leadership of Tacfarinas. The security needs of Africa meant that, despite its senatorial status, it was left with a legionary presence; indeed, it was the only such senatorial province when Augustus died in AD 14.

In all, therefore, the military side of imperial development was always high on the agenda during Augustus' long reign, although some areas were brought under control more successfully than others. It is clear, however, that the twenty-five legions which Augustus bequeathed to Tiberius, together with an approximately equivalent number of auxiliaries, represented the bare minimum for the task – or perhaps less than a reasonable minimum. It is little wonder, therefore, that the death-bed advice which Augustus gave to Tiberius, and indeed Tiberius' practice during his reign, left no room for adventurous innovation.

However, whilst the wars of conquest represented the means to achieve security and prosperity, the nature of that security was just as important. Amongst the reasons for Augustus' overall success, Tacitus includes the fact that the provinces welcomed what amounted to a new deal in which they were freed by Augustus' reforms from the effects of power struggles amongst the nobility and the corruption that had been endemic in a provincial system organised largely to cater for private profit.

As we have seen, much of the physical security of the Empire was in the hands of the legions and auxiliaries. Whilst these in some cases may, at first at least, have imposed a burden on local communities, it is clear that in general they came to constitute substantial markets and thus opportunities for local people, whether as farmers, industrialists or providers of services. Well paid as they were, the armed forces represented an important element in raising the level of provincial prosperity. There was also an important 'second line' in local defence; the communities of discharged veterans (*coloniae*) represented a major feature of Augustan policy in Italy and in the Empire. Between fifty and one hundred were established from the late 40s BC. Such communities, and others which had been granted citizen status (*municipia*), not only demonstrated the importance in the Roman system of the urban idea itself, but also made a major practical contribution in spreading the Roman way of life into the wider community through the system of attributing surrounding areas (*territoria*) to such towns.

A great deal depended upon the willing co-operation of local communities, as Rome provided insufficient manpower to undertake the whole burden of administration. As urban centres developed, the wealthy members of society took on administrative roles; the absence of salaries for such tasks meant that it was only such people who could undertake them. Local officials were usually elected or chosen by the wealthy from their own number; such officials, who went under different titles in different parts of the Empire, were modelled broadly on those of Republican Rome, or developed, where appropriate, from systems that had existed before. Such men also made up local senates and took on functions within the tax-collection system, the provision of public buildings and the organisation of local ceremonial.

There were a number of government policies which helped to foster the right atmosphere for such activities. The governors of provinces were now salaried and knew that to a greater or lesser extent they owed their position to an imperial patronage that was directed towards achieving efficiency and loyalty. Since such people no longer had to bribe or borrow their way into office, they were not faced with the need to recover their fortunes from unfortunate provincials. Similarly, the close contact, particularly in imperial provinces, between the governor and the *princeps* could be utilised to attract attention to a province's problems.

If provincial government became more professional, so too did financial administration. Rome depended upon imperial revenues, and it was therefore in everyone's interest to secure a system of taxation and organisation of imperial interests that was productive and fair. Regular censuses ensured that the basis for direct taxation was fair; further, the land tax and property tax could in appropriate cases attract immunities. Indirect taxes, such as harbour dues and death duties were also collected. The collection of these and the profitable operation of mining and farming on imperial estates were the responsibility of the equestrian *procurator Augusti* and his staff of junior procurators who were placed in every province. Promotion depended upon the successful carrying out of duties, thus again obviating the temptation to corruption.

During the Republic all tax collection had been handed over to profit-making companies (*societates publicanorum*), who were notorious for their rapacity. Indeed, during Mithridates' attempts to remove Roman rule from Asia Minor, the *publicani*, rather than senatorial officials, had been the especial object of venom. *Publicani* were still employed in the collection of indirect taxes, but in such a way as to deny them substantial profits. Obviously, now that provincials were having to finance a far smaller volume of Roman corruption, their prosperity increased, and with it the legitimate revenue and the willingness of such people to co-operate with Rome.

In such circumstances it was far easier to encourage civil or provincial pride, and Augustus cultivated this through the establishment of provincial councils (*concilia*) which had partly ceremonial functions, but could also initiate, for example, action against corrupt officials. Perhaps, however, the most effective binding force within communities and provinces was religion. The worship of the official Roman gods was conducted through the same officials as were responsible for local government. At the head of this religious system was the cult of *Roma et Augustus* – the imperial cult.

We can hardly expect that such arrangements as these pleased everybody; some provincials must have regretted the passing of their liberty. For most, however, the prospects of wealth and position which the provincial system afforded provided fuel to ambition. Few indeed will have been prepared to agree with the British chieftain, Calgacus, when he said: 'They create a desolation and call it peace.' The majority of provincials came to see that the *Pax Romana* of Augustus was much more than that.

8

The city of marble

The physical state of Rome could not be divorced from its moral, religious and political fibre; indeed Augustus' recognition of that fact is demonstrated in the high priority he himself gave to the record of his building work (*RGDA* 19–21). Horace, in fact (*Odes* III.6.1), specifically linked a religious revival with the rebuilding of the shrines themselves, and Augustus referred to the restoration of no less than eighty-two temples in the year 28 BC alone.

His building programme provided a means to put into a physical form his appreciation of the many facets of the *Respublica* and its restoration. A physical restoration in itself provided evidence that the rot had been stopped and that Rome was rising again; Augustus was by no means the only emperor to see the political virtue inherent in such a move. The building of a city worthy to be the centre of a great empire (Suetonius, *Life of Augustus* 28.3) was an important piece of propaganda in itself, because it showed the enhancement gained for Rome by a strong, united, pacified empire; this was a physical expression of *auctoritas* in Augustus' city. Again, rebuilding was not just a matter of aesthetics; it was also imperative for the sake of public safety and therefore for Augustus' role as patron and defender of the people. His famous boast that he had found Rome a city of brick and left it a city of marble is linked by Suetonius (*Life of Augustus* 28.3) with the idea of the enhancement of Rome's safety.

As we have seen, *pietas* was a central pillar in Augustus' restoration of Rome: the word carried with it the twin ideas of devotion to family and to the gods, and was thought to be worthy of emphasis both in the *Res Gestae* (*RGDA* 34.2) and on the coinage (*BMC* (Tiberius) 98). Indeed, the relationship of the imperial family with the idea of *pietas* is further emphasised if we accept the suggestion that Livia was the model for the personified *pietas* on a coin-issue of Tiberius. Not only was Augustus' *pietas* demonstrated in his attitude to his adoptive father and to the traditional gods of Rome, but it found expression through the building programme too.

In the *Res Gestae* a number of temples are mentioned, some of which may be said to hold more than a slight political significance. The temple of Quirinus linked Rome's first founder with its restorer; that of Magna Mater (the great mother, Cybele) represented a direct connection between Rome and Troy and between Augustus and Aeneas; nor will it have been lost on contemporary opinion that the great mother, brought to Rome during the second Punic War in response to a reading of the Sibylline Books, had waited two centuries for a temple of her own. Jupiter of *Libertas* commemorated Augustus' reconciliation with the nobility, whilst Jupiter Tonans was a favourite of Augustus himself, following his own escape from a lightning-strike whilst in Spain. Apollo too, Augustus' guardian at Actium, received a temple on the Palatine Hill, close to the house of the *princeps*. Augustus' interest in the family's place at the heart of Roman society is shown by his mention of the construction of temples to Vesta and to both the Lares and the Penates.

A significant part of his building effort was connected with his filial *pietas*. The *Forum Julium* with its commanding temple dedicated to Venus Genetrix, the tutelary deity of the *gens Julia*, was completed. In the *Forum Romanum*, the *Basilica Julia* was also completed; it represented the largest building of its type in Rome. Both the Forum and the Basilica also provided valuable public facilities, since traders and bankers both utilised them. The *Forum Romanum* was also the site of the temple of the deified Julius, standing opposite the speakers' platform (*rostra*), which was the heart of political activity during the Republic, and the senate-house, which Augustus also rebuilt.

In many ways, however, Augustan *pietas* achieved its most complete architectural expression in the *Forum Augustum* (2 BC); this, the third forum-area of central Rome, was again a public facility but summed up the Augustan idea of *pietas* in the great temple of Mars Ultor (Mars the Avenger), which presided over it. The god, of course, emphasised the success of Augustus as a

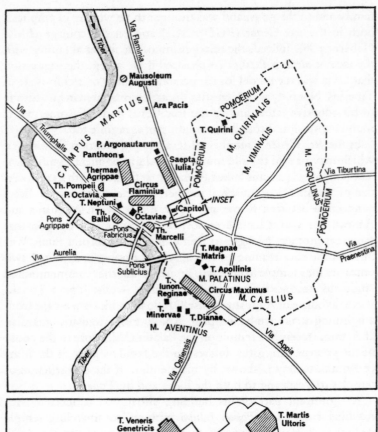

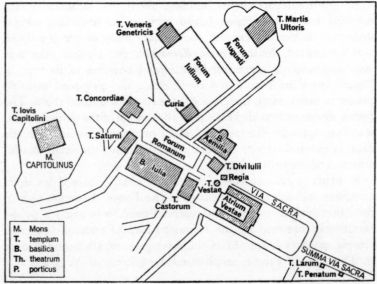

4 The city of Rome (from A. H. M. Jones, *Augustus*, London 1970)

war-leader and his role as the commander of the armies. But the temple's specific significance was as an offering of thanks to Mars for having allowed Augustus the ultimate expression of filial *pietas* in the avenging of Caesar's murder at the battle of Philippi in 42 BC. Thus filial and divine obligations came together in a single act of *pietas* which also emphasised the strength and unity of the *gens Julia* from Caesar, through Augustus, to his sons, Gaius and Lucius. It is ironic that it was this same year that saw the disgrace and exile of Julia for immorality.

We normally hear little of architects in Rome but a lot about those who put up the finance for building projects. It was an area of patronage that had long been exploited, particularly by those of the nobility who returned from foreign wars with money to invest. It is clear that the senatorial nobility will have considered their right to perform this function to be an integral part of *libertas* and *Respublica*, because it emphasised their power and at the same time the dependence of the mass of the population on them for the provision of such facilities.

Again, Augustus was able to turn this aspect of the *Respublica* to his advantage. His was the most pervasive patronage, and he was directly responsible for the erection of many of the buildings; nor should we overlook the fact that such a vibrant programme of public works provided employment on a long-term basis for large numbers of people who, without it, would have been unemployed and lacking in resources. It was an important aspect of the relationship between *plebs* and *princeps*, and it is worth noting that the later emperor, Vespasian (AD 69–79), declined to introduce labour-saving 'modern technology' into his building work as that would have defeated the object of providing employment.

Space was wisely left in the building programme for others of the nobility to contribute in the traditional way (Suetonius, *Life of Augustus* 29.4–5). Suetonius not only states the general principle, but picks out a number of specific examples of individuals who were encouraged to make themselves responsible for building and renovation, including Asinius Pollio, who was not noted for his co-operation with Augustus, Munatius Plancus, and two of Augustus' closest associates, Statilius Taurus and Marcus Agrippa. In the same way, the continued strength and unity of the family of the *princeps* (the *domus regnatrix*) were highlighted by buildings put up in the names of individual relatives – Octavia, Livia, Gaius and Lucius

Caesar, and Octavia's son, Marcellus; all the buildings concerned were public facilities or the scene of entertainments.

Naturally, the style of buildings was another significant concern in a restored Republic. Traditionalists had been extremely worried in the second century BC by the degree of Hellenisation that appeared to be overtaking Roman culture; Cato the censor in particular deplored the changing of old styles. Yet in architecture the availability of architects and materials, as well as money, from the east inevitably led to an element of Hellenisation in the design and execution of buildings. By most, this was accepted as perfectly reasonable, and the attitude of the Augustan age is aptly summarised in Horace's advice on Hellenisation as it affected poetry (*Ars Poetica* v.268f.) – that a study of all things Greek was an essential feature of the classical heritage of which Rome was a part.

The characteristic of Augustan architecture, as demonstrated by the contemporary practitioner Vitruvius Pollio, was a classical style that represented harmony between Greek and Etruscan antecedents – a stabilising, in fact, of a process of assimilating Greek ideas which had always been present in Italian architecture, but which had accelerated since the second century BC. This tasteful blending of the two would, it was hoped, satisfy traditionalists, whilst at the same time giving Rome the buildings that befitted her place in the world and taking advantage of new ideas and new technology.

Designs and plans of buildings were firmly rooted in Italian tradition; the Augustan temple standing on its lofty podium and approached by a single frontal flight of steps had advanced little since its Etruscan predecessors in towns like Tarquinia and Veii. However, the increasing use of marble (or, more often, marble cladding) or Italian substitutes for marble, such as travertine, and the employment of the Greek decorative orders – the Doric, the Ionic and, particularly in the Augustan age, the Corinthian – enhanced the Hellenised appearance of the building. Further, the columns, which were originally of timber, clad in terracotta, and restricted to the temple porch, were now often continued around the sides and rear of the shrine itself to give the appearance of the colonnade that normally surrounded Greek temples.

The public square (or piazza), familiar in many Hellenistic towns, was blended with the Italian forum. The forum had been in all probability originally an extension of the area in front of a temple where the people gathered to hear the pronouncements of the priests. This relationship of temple and public square was retained and is dramatically apparent in the *Forum Julium* and the *Forum Augustum*. But the marble pavements and colonnades of the Hellenised forum were adopted from their Hellenistic equivalents; in the case of the *Forum Augustum* the use of caryatids rather than columns was particularly bold. The public hall (or *basilica*) often made an appearance in the forum: this roofed extension of the forum had appeared in Hellenistic squares and had been introduced in Rome as early as the second century BC. The *Basilica Julia* (in the *Forum Romanum*) was the largest that Rome possessed to date, and with its use of cross-vaulting demonstrated how the technology of the Augustan age (in the form of the increasingly confident use of concrete) freed Roman builders from the constraints that had rested on both their Etruscan and Greek predecessors.

The buildings of the Augustan age were characterised by the abandonment of the use of older materials like sun-dried bricks; alongside the development of concrete was the growth of a huge industry of terracotta brick manufacture. Augustan and imperial buildings were predominantly of brick and concrete with an optional marble cladding.

As we have seen, it was highly important for the *princeps* to maintain and develop his patronal role with respect to ordinary people, and major buildings for public entertainment, such as theatres and amphitheatres, were a manifestation of this role. The Theatre of Marcellus was a landmark in this respect. Whereas the Greek theatre was constrained by reasons of technology to be constructed in a hollow or against a hillside, in Augustan Rome the bold use of concrete allowed the tiers of seats to be supported on an interweaving system of radial and concentric concrete vaults, and so permitted the structure to be erected anywhere. The Theatre of Marcellus became the exemplar of the great theatre and amphitheatre buildings to be constructed across the Empire over the ensuing four centuries.

The Roman nobility had always demonstrated its status by its houses; a lavish house had been one of the consequences of increasing wealth in the last two centuries of the Republic. In the second century BC, attempts had been made to legislate against the ostentatious use of wealth to promote a life of luxury. But these had been largely futile, and we know that great property-dealing went on when Sulla's proscription programme brought much property on to the market. Later, we are told gloomy stories by Plutarch of how, in the war between Pompey and Caesar, the

Republican leaders on Pompey's side spent their time dreaming of the houses which they hoped Caesar's defeat would bring on to the market.

Augustus made a point about domestic simplicity by preserving on the Palatine Hill the remains of very simple, thatched huts attributed to Romulus. The *princeps* himself was studiedly unostentatious in his domestic arrangements both in Rome and elsewhere in Italy; the *Villa Iovis* on the island of Capri, which acquired a probably undeserved notoriety in the time of Augustus' successor, Tiberius, was an essentially simple country retreat of the type enjoyed by many Roman nobles. Augustus' preference for simplicity, however, contrasted strongly with the views of many of his contemporaries, and Horace (*Odes* III.1.33ff.) complained particularly at the increasingly lavish private buildings appearing in fashionable areas such as the Bay of Naples.

The more modest examples of early imperial domestic architecture show again an element of Hellenisation whilst retaining strong links with tradition. Many Roman houses were built around a single courtyard, or *atrium*; beyond the *atrium* and opposite the entrance to the house was the *tablinum*, a room reserved for the father and which, because of the father's role as intermediary between the household and its gods, was a kind of shrine; the physical relationship between the *tablinum* and the *atrium*, from which the former was protected by a screen, recalls that between the Italian temple and the public area in front of it. The central feature of the *atrium* was a water-tank situated directly under a gap in the roof: early houses have no columns around the *atrium* tank, but late Republican and Augustan examples often have four or six columns around the tank and supporting the roof. The fact that the earlier type (without columns) was called *Tuscan*, and the later types (with columns) *Tetrastyle* and *Corinthian*, indicates clearly the contrast in origin. The most dramatic Hellenisation in domestic architecture, however, was the introduction of a very formal colonnaded garden (*peristylium*) beyond the *tablinum*; this replaced the less formal garden of earlier houses, which was probably used for supplying some of the family's food.

In all, Augustan architecture is best described as a tasteful compromise, in which the best of what was new and different found a place alongside the traditional. The result was an architecture whose combination of power and dignity was seen as a fitting expression of an imperial city and an imperial people.

Augustan architecture has left one particularly noble expression of the character of the age, and one which can properly be placed alongside the writings of Virgil, Livy and Horace. The Altar of Augustan Peace (*Ara Pacis Augustae*), built in the area of Rome known as the *Campus Martius* (Mars' Field), has no model in Roman architectural tradition; all of its antecedents were Greek.

The structure is simple: raised in the centre of the site is the Altar itself, and what survives of it carries decoration in the form of scenes from the procession that accompanied its dedication. It is the Altar's enclosure wall that is now principally of interest. Its interior carries the common Hellenistic decorative device of ox-skulls alternating with heavy garlands; the exterior surface, however, tells us much about Augustus' view of his role.

The external wall is pierced on its short sides by opposing entrance-ways; this therefore leaves for decoration the two long sides and the four panels flanking the entrances. In fact the whole enclosure wall is divided horizontally into two bands, the upper of which carries the documentary material, whilst the lower consists of acanthus fronds and spirals interspersed with swans. The choice of bird is not accidental, as the swan was sacred both to Venus, the tutelary deity of the *gens Julia*, and to Apollo, under whose especial protection Augustus regarded himself to have been.

The upper band has on the long sides two further processional scenes, one of which, now damaged, depicts Augustus himself and members of his family and entourage, including prominently Marcus Agrippa. Featured in this part of the procession are some very sensitive reliefs of the younger members of the Augustan family. The unity of the family with Augustus at its head is depicted as of paramount importance. The other long side – a continuation of the procession – carries representations of members of the senate. The two together portray the harmony of Augustus and the nobility which was the essential foundation of the restored Republic.

Flanking the entrances were four smaller panels (two of which are now substantially damaged) depicting significant scenes from the Augustan 'propaganda machine' which firmly identified the *princeps* with the traditional past. The two damaged panels depicted Mars with Romulus and Remus and with Roma. One of the other two panels depicts Aeneas sacrificing on reaching Italian soil – a reminder of Augustus' connections with the myths and legends of the past. The second shows the Italian fertility figure (Tellus/Italia) suckling children, which will have reminded observers of the Augustan policy of revitalising Italian agriculture (essential economically, socially and militarily) and of the clear commitment of the *princeps* to the concept of *Tota Italia* (Italy United) which he had defended at Actium. It will also have been a reminder of the same traditional simplicity that emerged from Virgil's *Eclogues* and *Georgics* and of the powerful relationship between Roman tradition and the *Pax Augusta* – a fitting expression of the reality of the restored Republic.

In general, therefore, and in detail, the Marble City emphasised the new beginning and the greatness of Rome's place and mission in the world. It also, however, shows that the new start was effected not by riding roughshod over all of Rome's past that was held in esteem and affection but by incorporating the past and thus demonstrating that the *Pax Augusta* and the restored Republic essentially represented the continuity of Rome's past greatness, now enhanced by the *auctoritas* of the *princeps*.

9

The succession

At the height of the tumultuous events of the civil war of AD 68–9, Tacitus (*Histories* I.15–16) puts into the mouth of the emperor Galba an oration, the main subject of which was the relationship between *libertas* and *Respublica* on the one hand, and the Principate on the other. Galba was not related in any way to Augustus, but all his predecessors – Augustus, Tiberius, Caligula, Claudius and Nero – were members of two families, the Julian and the Claudian, which Augustus had woven together by means of marriage-alliances. The period of the Julio-Claudian emperors (31 BC–AD 68) was seen by Galba to be at odds with the concept of *libertas*, because in effect Rome and the Empire had become the 'inheritance' of the united family.

Galba recognised the contrast between the *Respublica* and domination by one man, but also realised that the Republic could not manage without supervision. Thus, whilst he knew that the state's stability would not allow the removal of one-man rule, yet he felt that the fact that he was a 'chosen', rather than a hereditary, successor represented a significant move towards *libertas*; his own rise showed that the *princeps* could be chosen by his peers as a man of *auctoritas*, as Augustus himself had been chosen under the terms of the First Settlement of 27 BC.

The uneasy relationship between *libertas* and the Principate was long-standing (see Tacitus, *Agricola* 3.1); indeed it could be seen as essentially this which prevented reconciliation between Julius

71

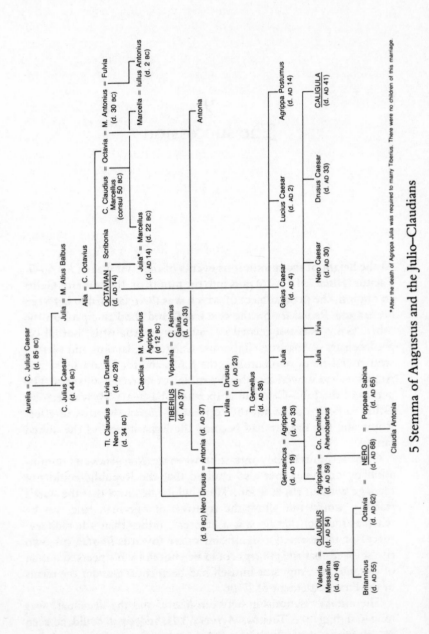

5 Stemma of Augustus and the Julio-Claudians

*After the death of Agrippa Julia was required to marry Tiberius. There were no children of this marriage.

Caesar and men like Brutus and Cassius. For Tacitus, the 'solution' hinted at in Galba's oration came to fruition with emperors such as Nerva (AD 96–8) and Trajan (AD 98–117), whose rise depended not at all on hereditary succession, but apparently on a choice made by the senate, on the recommendation of the incumbent *princeps*, from amongst those of their own number who had risen through the stages of the senatorial *cursus honorum*. The position of the *princeps* came to be seen as the pinnacle of the *cursus*, and this was the basis for the reconciliation of *libertas* and the Principate.

Later in the first century AD, therefore, it was perceived that the most obvious break with tradition presented by the Augustan regime lay in the emerging dynastic policy. However, as in other aspects of Augustus' policy, the divergence with past practice may in many ways have been more apparent than real. The *libertas* which obsessed the nobility of the Republic, and which has been described as their 'privilege' and 'vested interest', was founded upon the assumed right of sons to follow fathers up the steps of the *cursus honorum* to the consulate; the family's glory was thus enhanced. Nor were cruder forms of nepotism unknown in the Republic: when, in 133 BC, Tiberius Gracchus proposed the appointment of a land-commission, he ensured that its three members consisted of himself, his brother and his father-in-law. Further, the consolidation of factional pacts was invariably achieved with marriage-alliances.

Julius Caesar, however, put the matter into a somewhat tenser perspective; without doubt, the generality of opinion cast Marc Antony in the role of deputy to Caesar's leadership of his faction. Antony's behaviour in the immediate wake of the Ides of March showed that he was confident in that inherited role. However, Caesar not unnaturally wished also to bequeath his name, and C. Julius Caesar Octavianus was the beneficiary. It is impossible now to be certain precisely what Caesar intended to be the consequence of the act of adoption, though it is clear from the fact that Octavian would have joined his adoptive father on the Parthian expedition in 44 BC that Caesar meant at least to launch his new son on his career.

It is obvious that the murder of his adoptive father gave Octavian a filial duty to avenge Caesar's death. It seems likely, however, from his cultivation of Caesar's friends and opponents that Octavian, even in the summer of 44 BC, was looking further towards the primacy of the Caesarian faction. Antony, though generally dismissive of the youth who 'owed everything to his name', was anxious enough to

73

exchange his projected proconsulate in the Balkans for the nearer and more sensitive Cisalpine Gaul – a move that precipitated a chain of events that literally changed the world.

As a faction-leader in the wings, Octavian would hope to win the clientage that owed his adoptive father the most – the equestrian order, the army and the urban *plebs*. But to do so meant competition between himself, the leader now of Caesar's family, and Antony, the most senior adherent of Caesar outside the family. This clash within the faction of one who was a member of the Julian family and one who was not was a phenomenon that would appear again. The primacy of the Caesarian faction had effectively passed to Octavian by 39 BC, though legally he and Antony as *triumviri* remained on equal terms. Throughout the 30s, Octavian developed the Caesarian faction in its new mode – enhanced with many of the luminaries who had returned from self-imposed exile in Sicily with Sextus Pompeius, and established as the faction of traditional respectability and success. Finally, as Tacitus puts it (*Ann.* I.2.1), 'with Antony dead, the Julian party had no leader but Caesar'.

Octavian rose to the top as a faction-leader; the restoration of the Republic equated the leadership of the faction with the leadership of the state. Tacitus, however, was clear that Augustus' attempt to secure stability for his *Respublica* in the longer term represented a search for 'supports for domination'. There is no doubt, as Tiberius was to observe later (Dio LVII.8.2), that *dominatio* was a concept that sat uneasily alongside the *Respublica*. Significantly, Tiberius felt that he had a particularly difficult task in preventing the appearance of *dominatio* in his reign, because of the way he had come to power – that is, as the imposed choice of Augustus.

It is clear that not only did the search for a successor strongly imply domination but also the search itself released lurking tensions within the Caesarian faction – as it had done after Caesar's murder. Throughout his career, Augustus enjoyed the support of Marcus Agrippa as his right-hand man. However, loyal though Agrippa may have been, his ancestry was not sufficiently impressive to allow him to be a future leader of the Augustan *Respublica*; a plebeian of humble origin, as Agrippa was, would not be accepted by the nobility as *princeps*. Augustus could not allow himself to be swayed by sentiment in his search for a successor.

The first indication of a future leader of the faction came in the marriage in 25 BC of Augustus' daughter, Julia, to her cousin, Marcellus. It was thought at the time that the implication of this marriage angered and hurt Agrippa who consequently absented himself in the east. Marcellus, however, did not live long enough for the rift to deepen, and after his death in 22 BC a marriage was arranged between Julia and Agrippa. This did not point to Agrippa as the next faction-leader but was designed to achieve something more satisfactory, namely heirs who brought the family and the rank-and-file together. That Augustus thought this seems to be confirmed by his decision to adopt as his own sons the two oldest children of the marriage, who are known to us as Gaius and Lucius Caesar. The adoption did not apparently involve the physical removal of the two boys from their natural parents, now legally their guardians.

Even so, all was not to be plain-sailing; the death of Agrippa in 12 BC left the children without a guardian, and the widowed Julia was therefore married to Augustus' stepson, Tiberius Claudius Nero, who had served along with his brother, Nero Drusus, and with Agrippa in the campaigns in northern Europe. Tiberius' mother, Livia, despite her name, was born into the *gens Claudia*, and had originally married a Claudian (Tiberius Claudius Nero). Her enthusiasm for the success of the *gens Claudia* was strong and she recognised that the uncertainties caused by the death of Agrippa presented an opportunity for her son in the factional and dynastic politics of the Principate. Tensions clearly grew strong as the two young Caesars grew towards manhood and, with the self-effacement natural to him, Tiberius struggled with his role as husband and guardian – never forgetting his former wife Vipsania, whom he had been required to divorce in order to marry Julia.

In 6 BC, Augustus dramatically raised the public profile of Tiberius by associating him in the *tribunicia potestas*. Dio Cassius (LV.9) says that this was done to teach a lesson to Gaius and Lucius, who were not, it was said, developing a proper sense of responsibility. In disgust at what therefore amounted to an affront to his *dignitas*, Tiberius retired to Rhodes. So angry was Augustus at this desertion that, despite the ill-feeling caused within his family, he made it clear that Tiberius would not be welcome to return from his self-imposed exile.

Yet worse was to happen; in 2 BC, Julia, whose wild activities appear till then to have been known to everyone except her father, was exiled for involvement with a string of lovers whose names look sufficiently aristocratic to cause speculation that more was at stake. Tiberius, who did what he could from Rhodes to shield his wife from her father's anger, had now effectively lost his chief connection with Augustus' family – though he was of course still Livia's son. The promotion of Gaius and Lucius continued, and Tiberius' isolation made his position increasingly precarious.

However, what Augustus in his will referred to as 'a cruel fate' struck, and in two years, between AD 2 and 4, removed both Gaius and Lucius Caesar. Possibly this eventuality saved Augustus from mounting pressure from certain senators – if, that is, the rather curious affair of Cinna Magnus, lavishly embroidered by Dio (LV.14), is correctly dated to AD 4; for a threatened conspiracy on the part of this descendant of Pompey, whose position appears to have been supported by Livia, resulted in a new 'leadership package'. Tiberius had been allowed to return from exile in AD 2; two years later, along with Agrippa Postumus, the surviving son of Agrippa and Julia, he was adopted as a son of the *princeps*, changing his name to Tiberius Julius Caesar. Many said at the time that for Augustus the adoption of Tiberius was a last resort, and this receives some support from the fact that, simultaneously with his own adoption by Augustus, Tiberius was required to adopt as his son Germanicus, who was the son of Tiberius' brother, Nero Drusus. Germanicus was well-liked by Augustus, and had recently married Agrippina, the granddaughter of the *princeps*.

Tiberius received a new grant of *tribunicia potestas* and *imperium proconsulare*, which seems to have singled him out as the future leader of the Caesarian (or Julian) faction. As Augustus' health failed over the next ten years, Tiberius took on an increasing burden of administration, both at home and abroad. From AD 4, the way forward seems to have been settled, though the removal in AD 7 of Agrippa Postumus and his sister may provide an indication of continued family rivalry – as also may the rumours of Augustus' wish just before his death in AD 14 to be reconciled with Postumus.

In AD 14 Augustus died, and Tiberius was left, as his own behaviour showed, uncertain how to proceed. Clearly, the powers he held enabled him to rule, but he wanted it to appear that his role as leader of the Roman world derived partly from his factional leadership but principally from a recognition by the senate and people of his worthiness to supervise the workings of the *Respublica*. Most had come to expect that Augustus would be succeeded by a *princeps*. However, Tiberius, like Augustus before him, required that senatorial call to rule as the acknowledgement that his *auctoritas* was recognised. Apart from a few futile voices, it was now indeed admitted – grudgingly by Tiberius himself – that the *Respublica* did require permanent supervision and that Augustus' use of the factional principle was the most convenient and stable way of providing the continuity of that supervision.

It is clear, therefore, that in all but name the *Respublica* was now a hereditary monarchy, though Augustus' mention of alternative names outside the family (Tacitus, *Ann.* I.13) shows that in theory at least a continuity of *auctoritas* did not absolutely depend on the role of the Julian and Claudian families. In this sense, the objection to the hereditary principle and its infringement (by definition) of *libertas* looks forward to Galba's views in AD 69 and still further ahead to the accession of Nerva and Trajan in AD 96 and 98. There was, in other words, no ultimate conflict between *libertas* (as conceived by the Republican nobility) and the Principate.

Finally, there was a further element of continuity which was of great significance. The politics of the late Republic consisted essentially of the feuding of the rival factions of the *optimates* and *populares*; Caesar and Octavian had both emerged as *popularis* leaders. The eventual division of the imperial family into adherents of the Julians or Claudians effectively meant the continuity of the factional rivalry between *populares* (Julians) and *optimates* (Claudians). Tiberius' insistence on the involvement of the senate at his accession and subsequently shows his proximity to the old optimate viewpoint. Significantly, nothing could have been more characteristic of the *Respublica* than the feuding of *optimates* and *populares*; the continuation of this in a strong sense represented the continuity of the *Respublica*.

10

The legacy of Augustus

Over half a century separated the assassination of Julius Caesar and the death of Augustus in AD 14; during that time memories of the chaos of the late Republic had dimmed, and Augustus' restored Republic appeared to most to guarantee security and prosperity. Its government, as we have seen, was based on a combination of institutional features introduced by Augustus and the ability of the *princeps* to guide and persuade through his personal *auctoritas*. Tacitus and others, however, believed that Augustus' insistence on a dynastic succession was in conflict with the *libertas* that was traditionally a key factor in the working of the *Respublica*.

In the medium term, one legacy of Augustus was the line of successors from the Julian and Claudian families which was finally terminated by the pressures which led to Nero's suicide in AD 68. At that point, Nero's successor, Galba, who had come to power as the result of a military coup, argued (in a speech reported by Tacitus) that it was the dynastic nature of the succession that stood in the way of *libertas*, not the Principate itself. The variety of approaches adopted by the Julians and Claudians demonstrated that within the broad framework of the Augustan system many different styles of government might appear.

Caligula (AD 37–41) and Nero (AD 54–68) certainly appear to have believed in a much more direct form of monarchy than that employed by Augustus. Caligula is on record as having stated that his descent from the divine blood of Augustus afforded him complete freedom to rule as he liked; indeed he and Nero, it has been suggested, modelled their governing style on that of the Hellenistic monarchs who ruled in Asia Minor and the Middle East between the time of Alexander the Great and the absorption of those areas into the Roman Empire. In particular, what was perceived as the style of the Ptolemies of Egypt may have been the particular model for emperors who supported a direct form of rule, with the encouragement of the worship of themselves as gods. Inevitably, the disregard of the senatorial nobility that such a scheme presupposed fanned flames of discontent within that body, as being far removed from Augustan practices.

Of the other Julio-Claudians, Tiberius (AD 14–37) seems almost slavishly to have followed the Augustan model of co-operation between *princeps* and senate. However, his genuine attempt to continue this was undoubtedly vitiated by the fact that he had neither the reputation nor the diplomatic skills of his predecessor. It is clear too that Tiberius regarded himself as markedly inferior to Augustus, when he said that 'only Augustus was capable of undertaking the burdens of government', and followed this self-effacing observation by suggesting that power should be split between himself and others. Such a suggestion was dangerous in that it raised the idea of a weakness in the system that had not previously occurred to anyone.

Tiberius was acutely aware that Augustus was a difficult act to follow. Indeed, although his wishes were not heeded, Tiberius did at the beginning of his reign give instructions that the name, Augustus, should not be used of him because he was not worthy to hold it. Further, Tiberius was worried over aspects of his succession. In the first place, as Tacitus makes clear (*Ann.* I.7.10), the new *princeps* was embarrassed that he might be thought to have gained his position through dynastic intrigue rather than because he was thought to merit it. Second, he recognised the unique circumstances of Augustus' own elevation; he had won power for the faction which he dominated, and his immense *auctoritas* after Actium had made him unassailable. Further, the Republic was seen to be in need of reconstruction, and Augustus was able to proceed gradually along a path which led to reconstruction, but the nature of which suited his own temperament. Tiberius knew that his position was not like that, and his attempts to repeat in AD 14 the show of reluctant leadership engineered by Augustus in 27 BC ended in futility and frustration.

Claudius (AD 41–54), on the other hand, was a reformer, though of a less conservative type than circumstances and character had made Augustus. But Claudius wished to innovate and he wished to carry the nobility with him. Whilst, however, there is little doubt of the sincerity of his desire for co-operation, his reputation, character and behaviour led to his being despised and distrusted. In other words, he lacked the *auctoritas* of Augustus, and the nature of his reign showed clearly how critically necessary it was. Claudius' desire to maintain the importance of the senatorial and equestrian orders whilst persuading those bodies that they had to be much more ready to accept innovation in work and membership created a task in which a *princeps* of proven *auctoritas* might have stood a better chance of success.

Broader membership of the two orders was, however, inevitable in order to provide incentive and opportunity for the growing body of Roman citizens from the provinces. Where Augustus started and Claudius dreamed, later emperors carried on the process of reform; as a consequence, both senators and equestrians became even less concerned with governmental principles, and much more concerned with the administrative tasks that fell within their competence. Late in the first century AD, Tacitus, in his biography of Agricola, felt it perfectly natural to espouse this as an ideal within the Principate (*Agricola* 42.4).

History has seen one of Augustus' major achievements as the breaking of the vicious nexus between armies and their senatorial commanders which had destroyed the late Republic. He had done this, however, not by changing anything in principle, but by means of an *auctoritas* which was such that the armies willingly obeyed a commander who was recognised as the embodiment of the *Respublica*. It was the inevitable corollary of this solution that if later emperors were thought not to have the standing to merit this loyalty, then the loyalty might be withdrawn. The events of the civil war of AD 68–9 showed that the army could desert the *princeps* and offer its services to an alternative claimant. In this case, the dangers of the vicious nexus were just as real as they had been before Augustus came to power. It came to be accepted as early as Caligula's reign that financial bribery could prove an alternative, albeit temporary, to *auctoritas*. The Principate, then, very soon after Augustus was shown up as a form of government thoroughly dependent on its ability to maintain its armed backing, which should never be taken for granted.

Although the Augustan Principate did not solve as many problems as its contemporaries thought, Augustus himself remained a
by-word for success. Many emperors, through their statements and
their propaganda, claimed a political descent from Augustus; some
fostered the image of the 'New Augustus', whilst others echoed
Augustus' *pietas* in their own attitudes to his memory. It was
especially common for those who came to power after confusion
or aberration to place great emphasis on the memory of Augustus,
and to stress their links with the founder of the Principate. Galba,
following Nero, laid emphasis on the restoration of *libertas*, whilst
Vespasian after the civil war of AD 68–9 directed national attention
to the 'rebirth of Rome'. In AD 96, after another failed dynasty –
the Flavians, comprising Vespasian (AD 69–79), Titus (AD 79–81)
and Domitian (AD 81–96) – Nerva (AD 96–8) not only produced
a stream of propaganda that recalled Augustus, but issued a large
set of coins which, by commemorating 'the divine Augustus, my
father', sought to set his agenda for reconstruction firmly within an
Augustan context.

The ultimate legacy of Augustus was the broad sweep of stability
that the Roman world gained from 31 BC for four centuries and
more. Immediately, in the first century AD there was little that was
done that did not in some way imitate and follow Augustus Caesar.

APPENDIX I
Chief dates in the life and career of Augustus

BC 63	Birth of Gaius Octavius
58	Death of Octavian's father
44	Adoption by Julius Caesar; Caesar's assassination
43	Battle of Mutina; formation of Second Triumvirate with Antony and Lepidus
42	Battle of Philippi
41–40	Perusian War
40	Treaty of Brundisium; marriage of Antony and Octavia
39	Treaty of Misenum; return from Sicily of Republican 'exiles'
38	Marriage of Octavian and Livia
36	Defeat of Sextus Pompeius; Antony's loss of legionary standards to the Parthians
32	Antony divorces Octavia; Italy's 'oath of allegiance' to Octavian
31	Battle of Actium
30	Deaths of Antony and Cleopatra
28	Revision of the senate
27	First Settlement of the Principate
26–24	Augustus in Spain
25	Marriage of Marcellus and Julia
24	Episode of Marcus Primus
23	Second Settlement of the Principate
22	Death of Marcellus

22–19	Augustus in the East
21	Marriage of Agrippa and Julia
18	Revision of the senate: moral and social legislation
17	Augustus' adoption of Gaius and Lucius Caesar
16–13	Augustus in Gaul
12	Death of Agrippa; Augustus becomes *pontifex maximus*
12–9	Campaigns of Tiberius and Nero Drusus in Germany and Pannonia
11	Revision of the senate; marriage of Tiberius and Julia
9	Death of Nero Drusus
8	Death of Maecenas
8–7	Campaigns of Tiberius in Germany
6	Retirement of Tiberius to Rhodes
5	Gaius Caesar proclaimed *princeps iuventutis*
2	Augustus proclaimed *Pater Patriae*; Lucius Caesar proclaimed *princeps iuventutis*; disgrace of Julia

AD 2	Death of Lucius Caesar; return of Tiberius to Rome
4	Death of Gaius Caesar; adoption of Tiberius (and Agrippa Postumus); revision of the senate
6	Establishment of military treasury (*aerarium militare*)
7	Disgrace and exile of Agrippa Postumus and the younger Julia
9	Varus disaster in Germany
12	Tiberius made 'Co-Regent' (?)
14	Death and deification of Augustus; accession of Tiberius; murder of Agrippa Postumus

APPENDIX II
Provinces and armies in AD 14

This list indicates the division between imperial and senatorial provinces, the status of their governors (a = ex-consul; b = ex-praetor; c = equestrian *praefectus*) and the distribution between them of the legions.

Imperial provinces

(The *princeps* was legally the proconsul of these provinces, though his power was delegated to *legati Augusti*, *praefecti*, or *procuratores*)

Lusitania (b)	No troops
Hispania Tarraconensis (a)	Three legions (IV Macedonica; VI Victrix; X Gemina)
Aquitania (b)	No troops
Lugdunensis (b)	No troops
Belgica (b)	No troops
Germania Inferior (a)	Four legions (I; V Alaudae; XX; XXI)
Germania Superior (a)	Four legions (II; XIII; XIV; XVI)
Raetia (c)	No troops
Noricum (c)	No troops
Alpes Maritimae (c)	No troops
Sardinia/Corsica (c)	No troops
Dalmatia (a)	Two legions (VII Macedonia; XI)

Pannonia (a)	Three legions (VII; IX; XV)
Moesia (a)	Two legions (IV Scythica; V Macedonica)
Syria (a)	Four legions (III Gallica; VI Ferrata; X Fretensis; XII Fulminata)
Galatia (b)	No troops
Judaea (c)	No troops
Aegyptus (c)	Two legions (III Cyrenaica; XXII)

There were eighteen imperial provinces, containing twenty-four legions; of these provinces seven were governed by ex-consuls, five by ex-praetors, and six by equestrian *praefecti* or *procuratores*.

Senatorial provinces

(Regardless of *actual* status, all governors entitled *proconsul*)

Baetica (b)	No troops
Narbonensis (b)	No troops
Sicilia (b)	No troops
Macedonia/Achaea (b)	No troops
Asia (a)	No troops
Bithynia/Pontus (b)	No troops
Creta/Cyrenaica (b)	No troops
Africa (a)	One legion (III Augusta)

There were eight senatorial provinces, of which two were governed by ex-consuls, and six by ex-praetors. Only one of these provinces contained a legion, namely Africa.

Client kingdoms

Alpes Cottiae
Thracia
Cilicia
Cappadocia
Commagene
Armenia
Lycia
Mauretania

APPENDIX III
The sources for Augustus' Principate

Tacitus characterised the historiography of the Principate as being vitiated by two considerations. First, as government became progressively the business of one man, general knowledge of events and the thinking that lay behind them deteriorated. Second, the dominance of the *princeps* and in many cases his capricious character made it increasingly inevitable that writers would flatter the *princeps* whilst he was alive and vilify him once dead. In both these ways, the interests of posterity were compromised, and the truth was therefore hard to discover. It is likely, however, that the history of Augustus' reign was to a degree less affected by these considerations than was the case with the reigns of his successors.

Tacitus did not himself write a history of Augustus' Principate; his major works were first the *Histories* (covering the period AD 69–96, and published *c.* AD 106) and then the *Annals* (covering the period AD 14–68, and published perhaps *c.* AD 118, or possibly left unfinished at the time of his death); neither work has survived complete. Although the *Annals* are prefaced by a brief survey of aspects of Augustus' reign as they were relevant to an understanding of Tiberius, it does appear (*Ann.* III.24.4) that Tacitus later came to the conclusion that he would need to write a history of Augustus, but there is no evidence that he lived to do it. We can therefore only speculate on why he felt a history of Augustus to have become necessary; possibly it was due to a growing realisation that many of the difficulties faced by his successors had their roots in the form of government which Augustus had developed.

From the brief remarks which preface the *Annals*, it is clear that Tacitus saw Augustus' Principate as representing an increasingly centralised (and dominating) form of government; but at the same time, there was a general reliance on the continued tutelage of the Republic by the *princeps* – to the point, apparently, that many people could not contemplate Rome without him. Yet amongst the *nobiles*, as is shown by the speeches recorded after his death, opinion was divided as to whether Augustus should be viewed as Rome's hero and saviour or as the sinister and unscrupulous subverter of its government. In Tacitus' writings it is always important to distinguish between those sections in which he is making his own statements and those in which he is reporting the views of others. The 'Debate on Augustus' (*Ann.* I.9–10) falls into the latter category.

In a study of Augustus' life and reign, Tacitus and other historians will have had access to a wide variety of writers whose works (at least on the Augustan period) do not now survive. Livy, for example, took his great 'Roman Pageant' up to his patron's reign, and may not have been beyond casting a critical eye on contemporary events, as Augustus' reported reference to him as *Pompeianus* ('my Pompeian friend') may indicate. There were other writers too of independent spirit – Asinius Pollio who, according to Syme, was tolerated by Augustus as a 'privileged nuisance'; Cremutius Cordus, who was prosecuted in AD 25 for his praise of Brutus and Cassius; perhaps also Valerius Messala who fought for the Republican cause at Philippi. There is no indication that the freedom of speech of such writers was seriously infringed during Augustus' reign, though Cicero's correspondence with Octavian in 44 and 43 BC did not reach the edited collection of the orator's letters, and Augustus is said by Tacitus to have been moved late in his life to act against writers he regarded as libellous.

A great many people, particularly senators, wrote histories or memoirs, and these will have varied greatly in objectivity and usefulness; the Younger Agrippina (Nero's mother), for example, wrote an account of her family which may well have thrown light on the last decade or so of Augustus' life. The emperor Claudius wrote history, and his obvious admiration (as emperor) for the dynamism of Julius Caesar may imply criticism of the somewhat more conservative approach to politics of Augustus. Others are known to us only as names, as far as the writing of history is concerned, though in some cases other writings have survived – Servilius Nonianus (consul in AD 25), Aufidius Bassus, the Elder Seneca and the Elder Pliny. The last also wrote an account of Rome's German wars, which is cited on one occasion by Tacitus (*Ann* I.69.3). Both Augustus himself and Agrippa are also known to have written autobiographies.

Of contemporary writers, the sole major survivor is Velleius Paterculus whose two books of Roman history represent a summary of a much larger work. He was an equestrian officer and later a senator in the latter part of Augustus' reign, and lived through Tiberius' Principate, until *c.* AD 30, and was particularly interested in the northern wars in which he himself took part. Velleius is generally criticised as obsequious towards Tiberius and Sejanus (the prefect of the Praetorian Guard), though in fairness it should be said that he died before the truth about the latter's ambitions was fully understood and before the deterioration of Tiberius' last years. He is important for the preservation of some detailed information, and because he combines an admiration for the Old Republic and for the Augustan Principate – perhaps a contemporary indication of the compatibility of the two.

Although Augustus' own autobiography does not survive, we do have his official account of his reign (*Res Gestae Divi Augusti*), which was inscribed on bronze outside his mausoleum and of which Latin and Greek versions were made by a number of loyal cities throughout the Empire. The objective of the *Res Gestae* was to portray Augustus as a wise, modest and firm statesman and general under whose protection Rome, Italy and the Empire prospered. It is usually argued that the document, whilst not propagating untruths, is economical with the truth and often highly tendentious. Many inscriptions and edicts of the reign survive, of which the most important are perhaps the five 'Cyrene Edicts' of 7 BC which show Augustus intervening to order matters in a *senatorial* province. Another important official document which Tacitus certainly used for the reigns of Augustus' successors was the senatorial record (*acta senatus*); this must have been a source for many Augustan and senatorial speeches, as well as for official pronouncements which were channelled through the senate. A further source for the official version of certain events is provided by the reign's coinage.

Suetonius was a slightly younger contemporary of Tacitus, an equestrian who started life as a schoolmaster and latterly became a private secretary to Trajan and Hadrian before being dismissed in AD 122 for some impropriety. Suetonius had a major interest in compilation, and the majority of his listed works clearly indicate this. An orderly, rather than a critical, mind is the hallmark of his biographies of the emperors from Julius Caesar to Domitian; in these he treats his subjects' lives under a series of headings designed to cover antecedents, early life, personal and social habits, oddities and physical characteristics.

It is usually assumed that the preparation and writing of Suetonius' earlier lives were well advanced before his dismissal, as these contain far more detail than the later biographies. In particular, Suetonius makes full use of Augustus' correspondence, which enables him to put over a much more penetrating view of Augustus than of most of his successors. Particular faults of the biographer are the tendency to generalise from particular incidents, and the preference for personal anecdotes over discussion of constitutional or imperial matters. As a biographer, Suetonius could not be expected to produce a historical perspective; thus it is hardly reasonable to criticise him for failing to be something that he never intended to be.

The fullest account of Augustus' reign is also the latest – the history of the Severan senator, Dio Cassius, who reached a second consulship in AD 229. His work was effectively commissioned by Septimius Severus and written between AD 207 and 219. It is clear that he was a careful researcher who was prepared to exercise a critical judgement with respect to his sources. However, hard as Dio might try, he found it difficult always to distinguish between contemporary and earlier practices, which is particularly unfortunate in a historian who clearly desired to write a constitutional history. He is given to moralising and dramatising, which occasionally take him far beyond what could reasonably be corroborated by factual information. An obvious example of this is the long bedtime conversation which Dio reproduces (LV.14–22) between Augustus and Livia on the subject of the fault of one Cnaeus Cornelius Cinna Magnus, a descendant of Pompey. Such discursiveness is irritating, since it makes it difficult to determine whether or not Cinna was guilty of anything serious and to what the episode may relate.

In all, therefore, we have a varied collection of source material which provides plenty of information on Augustus' Principate – even if, for the various reasons stated, we have to be particularly careful in the way in which we employ it.

APPENDIX IV
Glossary of Latin terms

Auctoritas This concept, which was central to the Augustan Principate, is hard to render precisely; it means 'influence' and 'prestige', and embraces the idea of acquiring these through a combination of heredity, personality and achievement. Importantly, it implies the ability to patronise on a large scale.

Clementia This means 'clemency', or being generous to political adversaries: whilst it might on particular occasions be welcome in its effects, in principle it was a 'virtue' related to men of overwhelming (and thus, unwelcome) power, which could be denied as capriciously as it was exercised.

Colonia A city founded deliberately with a hand-picked population of Roman citizens, who were intended to act as a military reserve and as overseers of the neighbouring local population with a view to 'Romanising' it. This duty was rewarded by the concession of a degree of self-regulation of affairs. The planting of **coloniae** had a long history in the growth of Roman power in Italy and beyond, and was used during the Principate as a way of settling legionary veterans in sensitive areas. It differed from a **municipium**, a town which enjoyed a grant of Roman citizenship made to an *existing* population.

Consul The **consul** was the head of the executive branch of government during the Republic; two were elected each year, and were accountable to the electorate for their tenure of office. They presided over meetings of the senate and assemblies of the *populus* (whole people), and, until the late third century BC, regularly commanded the armies in battle, until this function was increasingly taken over by promagistrates (**proconsul, propraetor**). Under the Principate, whilst prestige still attached to the office, its importance came to relate more to the provincial and army commands for which it represented a qualification. Also under the Principate it became normal for the consuls who took office on January 1st (**ordinarii**), and who gave their names to the year, to resign midway through the year in favour of replacements (**consules suffecti**). This was a method of increasing the numbers of men qualified for senior commands.

Cursus honorum The ladder of office climbed during the Republic by senators in their quest for the consulship; it was subject to a number of organising laws (e.g. the **Lex Villia** of 180 BC, and a **Lex Cornelia** of Sulla), which laid down intervals between offices as well as the proper order for holding them. Under the Principate, the *cursus* remained in place, though a man's progress along it was affected by imperial favour (or the lack of it), and by the number of his legitimate children. The chief offices under the Principate (and ages of tenure) were as follows:

Office	Age
Vigintivirate (board of twenty)	18
Military tribune	21–2
Quaestor	25
Tribune of the plebs (often omitted)	
Aedile (often omitted)	
Praetor	30–5
Legionary commander (**legatus legionis**)	30+
Consul	37+
Proconsul or **legatus Augusti**	38+

Dictator Originally an office held for six months in an emergency, both consuls having agreed to abdicate. Sulla and Caesar, however, had longer tenures, and used the office and the protections it gave (e.g. freedom from tribunician veto) as the basis of a permanent control of government.

Dignitas This 'dignity' referred specifically to the holding of offices of the **cursus honorum**. It was, for example, an affront to Caesar's *dignitas* to be barred from competing for a second consulship, which by 50 BC he was entitled to do. Similarly, Tiberius took it as an affront to his *dignitas* that in 6 BC he was given tribunician power simply to annoy Gaius and Lucius Caesar.

Dominatio The state of being a master (**dominus**): the word originally and properly referred to the state of being a master of slaves, but is increasingly used to describe the position and behaviour of Julius Caesar and (by some) of Augustus.

Equites Members of the equestrian order were, during the Principate, Rome's second social class. Originally a rather disparate body, the order acquired coherence through its commercial activities following the expansion of the Empire from the second century BC. Companies formed within the order (**societates**) undertook (for profit) many tasks during the Republic of a civil service nature. Augustus re-organised the order so that it had a career structure consisting of posts in which similar tasks were carried out, but for salaries rather than profits.

Imperium The executive *power* bestowed on consuls and praetors during the Republic, through which they controlled the state. **Imperium** was tenable as it was defined – consular, proconsular. Augustus under the First Settlement controlled Gaul, Spain and Syria under a proconsular **imperium**, which was enhanced to superiority over others (*maius*) under the Second Settlement. He had a permanent residual **imperium**, which could be temporarily redefined to enable him to undertake other tasks, such as censorial duties.

Legatus Originally a man to whom 'assistant'-power was delegated; Pompey, for example, conducted his eastern campaigns with a number of **legati** in attendance. Under the Principate, a man became a **legatus** of a legion after the praetorship, but the term was usually employed of those to whom the emperor delegated *de facto* control of their provinces (**legatus Augusti pro praetore**), where the term 'propraetore' ('having the status of an ex-praetor') was used of ex-consuls in order visibly to subordinate them to the emperor's proconsular **imperium**.

92

Lex A law, which had been passed either by one of the assemblies (*comitia*) of the whole people (*populus*), or by the assembly of the plebeians (*concilium plebis*). Under the Principate, the participation of these bodies became a mere formality.

Libertas 'Freedom' had a wide collection of meanings in Rome, though that most frequently mentioned was the traditional freedom of the nobility to progress along the **cursus honorum** without undue interference from others. It was this **libertas** which was seen particularly as being in conflict with the principle of hereditary succession.

Municipium See above, under **colonia**.

Nobilis Literally, one who was 'known'; the **nobiles** (aristocracy) defined themselves as deriving from families which had reached the consulship in earlier generations, and regarded the consulship as virtually their birthright.

Optimates The **optimates** (or self-styled 'best men') during the Republic were those **nobiles** who felt that their factional dominance should be exercised primarily through an influential senate taking the leading role in government. It was effectively the **optimates**, with their blinkered view of Rome and its Empire, who forced Caesar and Pompey to war in 49 BC, and who were instrumental in Caesar's assassination five years later. During Augustus' reign, they and their descendants found the family of the Claudii more sympathetic to their political ideals than that of the Julii.

Patrician Traditionally the oldest part of Rome's aristocracy, who in the Republic's early days exercised the decisive role in government, maintaining a stranglehold through law and patronage over the political, military, legal and religious machinery of the state. The 'struggle of the orders' (traditional dates, 509–287 BC) gave more equality to rich plebeians, so that the real effectiveness of the distinction between the classes was eroded. Subsequently, the main factional groups (**optimates** and **populares**) each contained members of both classes. Augustus tried to revive the patriciate as the central core of his patronised aristocracy. Patricians were debarred from holding plebeian offices, such as the tribunate of the plebs and the plebeian aedileship.

Pietas The 'sense of duty' to gods, state and family that represented the traditional loyalties of the Roman noble, and which Augustus tried to exemplify and revitalise.

Populares The term, meaning 'mob-panderer', was coined by the **optimates** to describe the way in which their opponents appeared to devalue the senate's role in government, and to place their emphasis on manipulating the popular assemblies. The first notable **popularis** was Ti. Sempronius Gracchus (**tribune of the plebs** in 133 BC). Although the term fell into disuse after the Republic, nobles of this view tended to identify with the Julian family of Augustus, perhaps reflecting Caesar's position of primacy amongst the **populares** in the 50s and 40s BC.

Praefectus Under the Principate, the term 'prefect' was applied to various grades within the reformed equestrian order, from the commands of auxiliary army units to some of the highest officers in the order (**praefecti** of Egypt and of the Praetorian Guard).

Praetor This was the office second in importance to the consulship, although the **praetors** may in the earliest days have been the chief magistrates – **prae-itor** meaning 'one who goes in front'. From Sulla's time they had an increasing importance as the presiding officers in the courts (*quaestiones*); the post led on to legionary commands and/or governorships of second-rank provinces.

Princeps The term 'chief man' was favoured by Augustus as a form of address; it did not imply a particular office, but throughout the Republic had been applied to those who, in or out of office, were deemed to be prestigious, influential and disposers of patronage.

Princeps senatus A Republican term applied to the man who in terms of seniority (however conceived) was placed at the head of the list of senators, as Augustus was after the *lectio senatus* of 28 BC.

Proconsul The term was originally applied to a **consul** whose **imperium** had been extended beyond his term of office as consul to enable him to continue command of an army; by the second century BC, it was regularly applied to those who commanded provinces after their year of office in Rome: during the Principate it was used of the governors (whether ex-consuls or ex-praetors) of senatorial provinces.

Procurator The term was used of various grades of equestrian in the emperor's financial service – from the chief agents in the provinces, down to quite minor officials in their departments. They were officially distinguished by an adjective describing their different salary levels.

Respublica This word, often used emotively to describe the nature of the state which Augustus supplanted after Actium, means simply 'the public concern'. By definition, therefore, it would be negated by anyone with overwhelming and capriciously exercised powers (**dominatio**).

Senatus consultum The decree issued at the end of a senatorial debate which was not *legally* binding, but an advisory statement passing on the senate's opinion to those popular bodies responsible for making the final decisions and passing laws.

Tribune of the plebs Originally appointed, according to tradition, in 494 BC, the tribunes were officers charged with defending their fellow plebeians against injustices perpetrated by patricians. The decisive elements in their armoury were the *veto* by which they could bring any business (except that of a dictator) to a halt, and the *sacrosanctity*, by which all plebeians were bound by oath to defend an injured or wronged tribune. Gradually, the tribunes were drawn into the regular business of office-holding – almost, but not quite, part of the **cursus honorum**; their veto was employed increasingly as a factional weapon, and they became potentially powerful through their ability to legislate with the plebeian assembly without prior consultation of the senate. Under the Principate, little of their power remained, dominated as it was by the emperor's tribunician power (*tribunicia potestas*). Augustus, because he was by adoption a patrician, could not hold the office of tribune, though between 36 and 23 BC he acquired most of the powers of the office, and outwardly used them as the basis of his conduct of government in Rome. These powers served to stress his patronage and protection of all plebeians.

Triumvirate Any group of three men; the First Triumvirate of 60 BC was the informal arrangement for mutual assistance between Pompey, Crassus and Caesar; the Second Triumvirate of 43 BC was the legally-based 'office' of Octavian, Antony and Lepidus. The term continued to be used of occasional groups of three, and regularly of the three mint officials (**triumviri**, or **tresviri**,

monetales) and the punishment officials (**triumviri**, or **tresviri**, **capitales**), both of which groups were sections of the board of twenty, or vigintivirate, the first posts on the senatorial **cursus honorum**.

Select Bibliography

A great deal has been written about Augustus' life and Principate, and only a few of the most important works can be mentioned here.

Cambridge Ancient History, vol. X (Cambridge 1934), chs 1–18: this is a thorough survey, though some of the chapters on the provinces are rendered somewhat out of date by progress in archaeology.

Ancient sources

P. A. Brunt and J. M. Moore, *Res Gestae Divi Augusti*, Oxford 1967.

V. E. Ehrenberg and A. H. M. Jones, *Documents Illustrating the Reigns of Augustus and Tiberius*, Oxford 1955.

C. H. V. Sutherland, *The Roman Imperial Coinage*, vol. I, London 1984.

Dio Cassius, *Roman History* (*The Reign of Augustus*, translated by Ian Scott-Kilvert, Penguin Classics) London.

Suetonius, *The Life of Augustus* (in *The Twelve Caesars* translated by Robert Graves, Penguin Classics) London.

Tacitus, *The Annals of Imperial Rome* (translated by Michael Grant, Penguin Classics) London.

Velleius Paterculus, *Roman History* (translated by F. W. Shipley, Loeb Classical Library).

Modern authorities

A. Boethius and J. B. Ward-Perkins, *Etruscan and Roman Architecture*, London 1970.

G. W. Bowersock, *Augustus and The Greek World*, Oxford 1965.

J. M. Carter, *The Battle of Actium; the Rise and Triumph of Augustus Caesar*, London 1970.

A. M. Duff, *Freedmen in the Early Roman Empire*, Oxford 1928.

D. C. Earl, *The Age of Augustus*, London 1968.

E. Fraenkel, *Horace*, Oxford 1957.

M. Grant, *From Imperium to Auctoritas*, Cambridge 1949.

M. Grant, *Roman History from Coins*, Cambridge 1956.

M. Hammond, *The Augustan Principate*, Harvard 1933.

A. H. M. Jones, *Studies in Roman Government and Law*, Oxford 1968.

A. H. M. Jones, *Augustus*, London 1970.

F. Millar, 'The Emperor, The Senate and the Provinces', *JRS* LVI (1966), 156–66.

F. Millar, *The Roman Empire and its Neighbours*, London 1966.

R. M. Ogilvie, *The Romans and Their Gods*, London 1970.

B. Otis, *Virgil, A Study in Civilised Poetry*, Oxford 1964.

H. M. D. Parker, *The Roman Legions*, Oxford 1928.

M. Rheinhold, *Marcus Agrippa*, New York 1933.

T. Rice Holmes, *The Architect of the Roman Empire*, Oxford 1928.

E. T. Salmon, 'The Evolution of the Augustan Principate', *Historia* V (1956), 456–78.

F. Sear, *Roman Architecture*, London 1982.

D. C. A. Shotter, 'Principatus ac Libertas', *Ancient Society* IX (1978), 235–55.

G. H. Stevenson, *Roman Provincial Administration*, Oxford 1939.

C. H. V. Sutherland, *Coinage in Roman Imperial Policy 31 B.C.–A.D. 68*, London 1951.

R. Syme, *The Roman Revolution*, Oxford 1939.

R. Syme, *The Augustan Aristocracy*, Oxford 1986.

L. R. Taylor, *The Divinity of the Roman Emperor*, Middletown 1931.

P. G. Walsh, *Livy: His Historical Aims and Methods*, Edinburgh 1961.

G. Webster, *The Roman Imperial Army*, London 1985.

Ch. Wirszubski, *Libertas as a Political Idea at Rome*, Cambridge 1950.

G. Williams, 'Poetry in the Moral Climate of Augustan Rome', *JRS* LII (1962), 28–46.